W9-AEA-551

Myth and Meaning, Myth and Order

Myth and Meaning, Myth and Order

Stephen C. Ausband

MERCER UNIVERSITY PRESS ● MACON, GEORGIA

ISBN 0-86554-089-6

All books published by Mercer University Press are produced
on acid-free paper that exceeds the minimum standards set by the
National Historical Publications and Records Commission.

Library of Congresss Cataloging in Publication Data
Ausband, Stephen C., 1943-
Myth and meaning, myth and order.

Includes bibliographical references and index.
1. Mythology.   2. Myth.   I. Title.
BL311.A97   1983   291.1'3   83-5478
ISBN 0-86554-089-6

Table of Contents

PREFACE   ix

ACKNOWLEDGMENTS   xiii

1—MYTH AND MEANING   1

2—THE BREAKUP OF SYSTEMS   23

3—REACHING FOR MYTHS   43

4—BEGINNING AND RETURNING   59

5—LOOKING OUTWARD: THE MYTH OF THE STATE   77

6—LOOKING INWARD: THE MYTH OF THE SELF   91

7—MYTH AND ORDER   107

Dedication

To Melinda, who knows these things.

We live in an old chaos of the sun,
Or old dependency of day and night,
Or island solitude, unsponsored, free,
Of that wide water, inescapable.
Deer walk upon our mountains, and the quail
Whistle about us their spontaneous cries;
Sweet berries ripen in the wilderness;
And, in the isolation of the sky,
At evening, casual flocks of pigeons make
Ambiguous undulations as they sink,
Downward to darkness, on extended wings.

—Wallace Stevens

Preface

To WHAT EXTENT is the student of mythology a mere dealer in antiquities, a kind of archaeologist of narratives who dusts off and preserves, as for museum display, the tales and traditions of the past? The answer, I believe, depends on if he deals exclusively with ancient cultures—that is, without being aware of the role mythology plays in any civilization.

For the past five decades, many of the major treatises on myth and ritual have attempted to deal with the crucial function of myth as an expression of the order a society perceives in itself and in the world at large. A thorough study of various mythological traditions demonstrates that societies have depended on radically different mythic traditions because of some very basic differences in their outlooks. Underneath the diversity, however, there is a constant and uniform need—a uniformly human need—to find a way of dealing with the unending human questions about necessity, chance, purpose, and the meaning of life.

It was the psychologists, especially Freud and Jung, who did the most early in the twentieth century to kindle widespread and popular interest in the use of mythology. Freud, especially in books like *Totem and Taboo* and *Interpretation of Dreams*, suggested that myths arose out of and appealed to man's subconscious mind, expressing the hopes and fears of prehistoric people. Since the most basic of these hopes and fears have not changed very much, the old mythic forms still have the power to move the modern mind. Carl Jung, who was in many ways as avid a student of mythology as he was of psychology, believed that the tendency to think in terms of the forms (he called them archetypes) is an inherited trait passed along from one generation to another as a kind of storehouse of memories.

In the twentieth century, the study of myth has attracted the attention of anthropologists, sociologists, psychologists, philosophers, and literary scholars. While each field has its own approach or set of approaches to the general subject of mythology, experts in every field are united in their conviction that, in the first place, the mythology of any society is an expression of the standards and the values peculiar to that society, and, in the second place, there exist recurrent patterns in mythology which are shared by virtually every society.

Unfortunately, many modern men and women—modern American men and women in particular—know only a little about the mythology of other civilizations. They also know only a little about the languages, social customs, literature, and art of other civilizations because modern education tends to stress the contemporary and the topical at the expense (sometimes to the exclusion) of what used to be called "the classics." Therefore, as James Burl Hogins complains, "stories that used to be part of every childhood have been supplanted by modern 'relevant' tales, such as accounts of trips to the dentist or narratives of life in the ghetto."[1] This does not mean, of course, that modern man lives without myths; it only means that he is likely to be ignorant of the myths of other people and, as a consequence, ignorant of the way mythology works in any society. Myths and rituals are, as Mircea Eliade and Joseph Campbell

---

[1] "Introduction," *Literature: Mythology and Folklore* (Chicago: Science Research Associates, Inc., 1974), p. 1.

and a host of other mythologists have demonstrated, very much a part of our daily activities, of the way we see ourselves, and of the way we order the world around us.[2]

Some myths have a basis in fact. (According to Euhemerus, even stories about the gods may be in part factual, based on the exploits of outstanding mortals who later became elevated to the status of deities.) Certainly Charlemagne existed as a historical figure, and perhaps Baligant and Roland and Ganelon did too. *Beowulf* contains names (such as that of Hygelac) and refers to events (such as Hygelac's raid on the Francs) which are demonstrable parts of European history. Troy was certainly real enough; it even looked very much the way Homer said it looked in his descriptions of it in the *Iliad*. But these links with the historical past, however interesting they may be, are trivial in comparison with the larger role of myths as agents of truth. One might paraphrase here the distinction Aristotle made between the truth of history and the truth of literature. Whereas history deals with facts and circumstances about specific individuals, mythology deals with that which is true for all individuals. While the myths change as societies change, the needs for myth and the uses of myth remain constant. To explore those needs and uses in modern society is the purpose of this book.

The first two chapters of the present work provide an overview of the function of myth, as well as deal with the problem of the breakdown of traditional mythic systems in the West. The five chapters which follow consider the attempts of Western (and, again, particularly American) man to arrive at some sort of workable mythology, a comprehensive system of tales and traditions to help him find order even in the face of the chaos that constantly threatens him. I rely often on selections from or discussions of various literary works, especially works from the nineteenth and twentieth centuries, in dealing with the dilemma of modern man and his myths, but I do not intend the book as a work of literary

---

[2]See especially Eliade, *The Sacred and the Profane: The Nature of Religion* (New York: Harcourt, Brace, 1959) and *Man and the Sacred: A Thematic Source Book of the History of the History of Religions* (New York: Harper and Row, 1974).

criticism. It is instead a brief attempt to define and examine some of the common myths with which we live and through which we sometimes find meaning and order in life.

Acknowledgments

I SHOULD LIKE TO thank my colleagues on the Faculty Development Committee and the administration at Averett College for granting me the sabbatical leave that made much of the work on this book possible. I am also grateful to my wife and to faculty members in several departments for reading and commenting on parts of the manuscript, for providing encouragement and ideas, and for listening patiently to me and talking with me about many of the matters covered in the following pages. Finally, I want to express my appreciation to Rolv Lind for the wealth of information he made available to me on the myths and folklore of the Shona people of Zimbabwe.

—Stephen Ausband

Chapter 1

Myth and Meaning

> *For those in whom a local*
> *mythology still works, there*
> *is an experience both of accord*
> *with the social order, and of*
> *harmony with the universe.*
> —JOSEPH CAMPBELL

ANY CONSIDERATION of mythology and its role in the lives of modern men and women must begin with some sort of definition of the term. We tend to think of myths as stories that other people believe or once believed to be true, but that are not really true. This has been the case in all societies. Sir Walter Raleigh, an avid student of classical mythology, embraced a series of beliefs regarding the origin of the universe, the existence of demonic spirits, and the nature of non-European people that most twentieth-century college students would regard as mythically based. That these same students are unable to see their own beliefs as mythically based is not perversity; it is human nature. Human beings need to find some sort of order in their world, and the system of tales and traditions we call mythology is a primary way of reinforcing that order. Mere observation tells us that the sun rises from a certain direction and runs a certain course across the sky. Myths arose to tell us why, relating the movement of the sun to the power, the governing will of the universe. Observation tells us that man dies and that his death is exactly like the deaths of other animals. Myths were created to deal with the question of what happens to the invisible spark, the mind or soul, that wonders about death while the body is still alive. Observation and reflection tell us that man seeks control and power over certain aspects of his world. Myths tell us how that power and control may be won or lost.

Man's desire for order, his absolute and dogged insistence on order, is the foundation of his humanity. He names things, and he ranks and orders them as he does so. Adam's first job on waking in the garden was to give things their names, and as he did he made them manageable and discovered—or imposed—an order on them. Myths are tales which demonstrate the order that a man or a society perceives in natural phenomena. It is the role of mythology to make the world coherent and meaningful by demonstrating or imposing order on it. No society has existed that did not need some sort of structure, a system of belief, by which it could ask and answer questions about its relationship to the universal. Myths die as societies change, but the need for the myth does not die because man's need for order does not change or die.

We can see this need all around us, reflected not only in our daily lives, but in our literature and our art as well. When a society outgrows or for whatever reason abandons belief in a coherent mythic system—like, for instance, the traditional Judeo-Christian mythology involving a benevolent God and a malevolent Satan—confusion abounds until the society can find something to take the place of that which was lost. Certainly much of the literature and the art of the modern period is a testimony to the confusion of modern life; we are shown, again and again, the problem of man who has, as William Barrett put it, "lost his anchorage in the eternal."[1]

One possible result of the confusion, as Nietzsche was quick to tell us, is nihilism. One could assume that because the symbol, the myth, was

---

[1] For an excellent discussion of the relationship of modern art and literature to the perceived breakdown of order and the rise of the existentialist movement, see especially the third chapter, "The Testimony of Modern Art," in William Barrett's *Irrational Man: A Study in Existential Philosophy* (Garden City NY: Doubleday, 1962), pp. 42-65.

false (that is, it was not true to observable phenomena), the thing that it symbolized was also false, a foolish and antiquated holdover from a more childish age. The *reductio ad absurdum* of this assumption would be the conclusion that there are no moral directions at all, that nothing is either good or evil. Generosity is not good and genocide is not evil; they are simply facts, things, the way flowers are things or sunrises and sunsets are things. This would be a very hard decision to come to, for it would leave one no place at all to stand and say, "This is good," or "This is bad." The very idea of praising or damning any action on the basis of the morality involved in it would become ridiculous. That is why true nihilists have always been rare, even in the most radical ages, when major theological or societal myths have crumbled. Obviously, no society, however small, has existed without some sort of code of behavior, even in the most chaotic times.

On the other hand, nihilism can, in certain circumstances, be a very convenient decision to come to, for one no longer has to weigh his own actions in terms of good and evil, right and wrong. No one has seen this more clearly than Albert Camus, whose Caligula is a perfect example of a man completely free from a sense of duty, responsibility, or conscience—free, in a sense, from his gods and his myths. Nothing is bad except self-denial, so Caligula denies himself nothing, including the opportunity almost to bathe himself in human blood. Camus shows us a man who becomes a monster because it is, after all, not an illogical thing to do.

More common than nihilism is the assumption that, while there may be no gods and no devils, real moral directions do exist. They are not unchanging or sacrosanct directions because they are made by human societies, and human societies change. Nevertheless, because a human being must live and act in a world filled with other human beings, the standards are just as real as if they had been graven on stone tablets by some god's fiery finger. It only remains, in the face of the loss of a coherent mythic system, for the individual to find and embrace those standards that will make his life orderly and decent and bearable in relation to the lives of other people. In the process, he might go about creating (through art and literature usually) a new kind of mythology to reinforce his chosen beliefs.

Ernest Hemingway saw this second alternative very clearly; it is almost the only thing he ever really wanted to write about. (Hemingway got sidetracked sometimes and wrote a great deal about less pressing things, but he often wrote about this sense of loss and the reaction to it. See especially "A Clean, Well-Lighted Place" and *The Sun Also Rises* for examples of his handling of the theme. Before Hemingway, the American author who saw it most plainly was Mark Twain—which may be one reason why Hemingway said that Twain was the greatest American author before himself.) In "A Clean, Well-Lighted Place," the older waiter knows that all is *nada y pues nada;* that there is no God, no Satan, no reward or punishment, and no reason—not even any reason—to life in the universe. But because there is no reason, no order, a man must create reason and order and stand for them and in them so as to be worth something in his own eyes. The rules he chooses to live by may be artificial and arbitrary, like the rules of the bullfight or of the hunt. A man either stands for something—even something arbitrary and artificial and perhaps even stupid—or he stands for nothing, for chaos, for what Hemingway called "messiness."

There is a lot of talk in Hemingway criticism about "the code." The code was simply what people had to make when their gods all died and they lost their sense of direction. According to Jake Barnes (who lost not only his religion but his manhood sometime after 1914) and Brett Ashley (who never lost anything, especially a sense of order, because she never had a sense of order to begin with), "It's sort of what some people have instead of God."

The most pressing human need may indeed not be the need for food but the need for order. This explains why stranded people have starved to death rather than eat the flesh of fellow stranded people, even though the flesh could have kept them alive. When we read of acts of necessary cannibalism such as that among the survivors of the plane crash in the Andes Mountains years ago, we read also of the desperate attempt to make the act somehow decent and orderly, even religiously sanctioned. It was not enough that the act was sane and logical; it had to be ethical—it *had* to be—or, if we can believe Piers Paul Anderson, there might have been no survivors. There were no Caligulas on the plane.

Myths work by demonstrating order. They are true in the sense that they are satisfactory demonstrations or representations of a perceived order and are therefore often believed by a society to be more or less factual. I say more or less because I think it has seldom been the case that all myths in a mythology were accepted by all the people of that mythological tradition as being absolutely, factually true. It was not necessary, for instance, for the Greeks who first saw the *Orestia* of Aeschylus performed sometime in the fifth century, B.C., to belive in the physical, tangible existence or the erinyes or furies. They understood guilt and fear, they believed that the gods, the powers of order in the universe, could punish a man for the horrifying crime of matricide. They believed in the historicity of the house of Atreus, they believed in the gods, and so they believed in the myth much as Aeschylus presented it in a dramatic and artistic form. The haunting of Orestes by the erinyes was a part of the myth that could be interpreted more or less literally, according to the disposition of the individual playgoer. The important thing is that the story on which Aeschylus based his drama was a living part of the tradition of the Greeks; it was, in that sense at least, true.

Similarly, while very few modern Christians would say they believe in the factual nature of every tale in the Bible (the story of Balaam's talking ass comes to mind, as does the tale of the tower of Babel), many of the stories—some of them no less farfetched, to the objective mind, than the tale of Zeus taking the form of a swan and raping Leda—are believed.[2] When a significant number of tales in any mythological tradition are

---

[2]For some of the early church fathers, a way out of the dilemma posed by certain crude or barbaric or apparently pagan practices recorded in the Old Testament was the doctrine of "condescension," according to which God allowed certain imperfections to remain temporarily in the religion of the Jews.

accepted as true and as important demonstrations of the order that a society perceives, then the mythology can be said to be vital. When a tradition consists of tales that most people believe to be untrue, that do not stand at once as both factual and as demonstrative of a perceived order, then the tradition is dead.

The psychoanalyst Géza Roheim made an interesting distinction between myths and folktales. Roheim said that myths are narratives in which the actors are generally divine (occasionally they may be human), which have a definite locale, are part of a creed, and are believed by the narrator. Folk tales, on the other hand, involve characters who are human (the hero is almost always human, although his opponents may be supernatural), have indefinite settings, and are purely fiction and not intended to be anything else.[3] The most important point in Roheim's distinction, it seems to me, is the last one. Whether they are believed to be absolutely factual or not, myths are always treated seriously by the society for which they form part of a living tradition. To sum up a definition, then, one might say that myths are tales that are accepted, on the whole, as either true to historical fact or as reinforcing and demonstrating a society's understanding of the truth about natural phenomena, and which are treated seriously by most members of the society.

Interest in a study of mythology is not new; at least by the sixth and fifth centuries, B.C., men were discussing and analyzing older mythic beliefs and debating the use and nature of mythology. The sophisticated philosophers and mathematicians of ancient Greece, men like Thales, Theagenes of Rhegion, and Pythagoras, looked at some of the more fantastic tales from Hesiod with a jaundiced eye. These men tended to interpret the tales as broad allegories in which the various gods and goddesses served as poetic devices suggesting specific aspects of human nature or of natural phenomena. One finds an interesting variation on this allegorical approach in the tragedies of Euripides, who seemed to regard elements in the tales as emblematic of the passions which govern

---

[3]"Myth and Folktale," *American Imago* 2 (1940): 266.

man. In the *Bacchae*, for instance, Euripides reworks the tale of King Pentheus's opposition to the worship of Dionysus and the subsequent murder of Pentheus at the hands of maenads led by his own mother, Agave. Because Euripides concentrates on the repressed individuality and sexuality of women in Greek society, the play is as much about the conflict between repression and expression of desire and emotion as it is about a god named Dionysus and a man named Pentheus. Phillip Mayerson's observations on the three great tragedians of ancient Greece are worthwhile: he notes that Sophocles took his tales directly from the sources (Homer and Hesiod, mostly) and gave them a fairly straightforward treatment in the tragedies. Aeschylus saw a developing moral order in the universe. This order finds expression in works like the *Orestia* in which the young god Apollo gains sway over the older, barbaric forces; the punishing erinyes become eumenides, guardians of justice; and ordinary people become civilized Greeks. Euripides is the most psychologically oriented of the three playwrights, using the ancient tales over and over again to explore the forces and passions that rule human behavior.[4]

While some Greek philosophers saw the tales as allegorical, the fifth-century historian Herodotus made an exhausting study of various myths as corrupt versions of historical accounts. The most pervasive and influential form of interpretation along these lines comes from a Messenian philosopher named Euhemerus (from whose name we get the word Euhemerist). According to Euhemerus, the various gods and goddesses were once human beings—kings, queens, sages, lawgivers—who were so venerated by their people that they became elevated to the status of deities several generations after their deaths. Raphael Patai points out that Euhemerus, who wrote just after the time of Alexander the Great, may have been influenced by Alexander's "consciously emphasized parallelism between his expeditions to India and the triumphant procession

---

[4]Phillip Mayerson, *Classical Mythology in Literature, Art, and Music* (Waltham MA: Xerox, 1971), p. 10.

through the same remote part of the antique world attributed by myth to Dionysus."[5] At any rate, Euhemerism became an important way of looking at myth in future centuries. Many of the early Christian fathers, including Clement of Alexander (c.150-c.220) and St. Augustine (354-430), were Euhemerists, and it is probable that their approach made possible the survival of the pagan Greek and Roman gods into the Renaissance. After all, good Christians, even in the most desperate and dogmatic years of the medieval period, should find no fault with good pagan kings and sages, even if Error had made them into gods.[6]

In the late Middle Ages and early Renaissance, heightened interest in classicism often prompted writers to look for parallels between pagan morality (as it was revealed in myths) and church doctrine; many went so far as to view the earlier tales as corrupt or clouded versions of their own traditions. Giovanni Boccaccio, whose works influenced other writers for hundreds of years after his death, was an avid student of classical literature, adopting for his own use stories like that of Troilus and Cressida (which he got from a medieval version of a very slight incident related by Dares Phrygius). Boccaccio published a lengthy treatise called *Genealogy of the Gods* which attempted to show the moral, Christian nature of the pagan myths and to reconcile, in a sense, classical paganism with fourteenth-century Christianity. Dante put Vergil in the *Divine Comedy* as a guide through the Inferno and Purgatory, right up to the gates of Heaven. (Dante was not alone in regarding Vergil as preeminent among the pagan moral philosophers. Vergil's *Eclogues* were even said to contain a prophecy of the birth of Christ.) For obvious reasons, one of the most popular figures from the classical tradition was Prometheus, whose

---

[5]Phillip Mayerson, *Myth and Modern Man* (Englewood Cliffs NJ: Prentice-Hall, 1972), p. 12.

[6]Ibid., p. 13. For discussions of medieval Euhemerism, see especially Jean Seznec, *The Survival of the Pagan Gods* (New York: Pantheon Books, 1953) and J. D. Cooke, "Euhemerism: A Medieval Interpretation of Classical Paganism," *Speculum* 2 (1927): 396-410.

suffering for mankind made him a type or prefiguring of Christ. Similarly, the fall of Phaeton could be regarded as a lesson on the consequences of pride or even as a version of the fall of prideful Lucifer.[7]

Throughout the seventeenth and into the eighteenth century, there were numerous efforts to reconcile the tales of other traditions with the Judeo-Christian heritage. Crude as some of these efforts were, they were the beginning of the study of comparative mythology. Reports of the religious beliefs of the New World Indians provided extremely fertile ground for Europeans interested in comparing their own traditions with those of other people. An influential work by Pere Joseph Lafitau entitled *The Customs of the American Savages Compared to the Customs of the First Ages* (1724) compared the beliefs of the Iroquois with those of ancient civilizations and concluded that all the traditions were merely corruptions of a "natural" religion, coming from divine inspiration, and that Christianity was a correction of earlier errors in interpretation. Lafitau stated, "This corruption, however, no matter how enormous it was, is not so general that one cannot find in the depths of this corrupted religion principles contradictorily opposed to the corruption, principles of a strict morality that calls for an austere virtue, that is an enemy to disorder, and that supposes a religion holy in its origin and holy before it was corrupted." Furthermore, Lafitau goes on to discuss finding "vestiges of the most holy trinity in the mysteries of Isis, in the works of Plato, and in the religions of the Indies, of Japan, and of the Mexicans."[8] A few years after the appearance of Lafitau's work, a growing cult of sentimentalism and primitivism made some Europeans anxious to discover a noble savage in every primitive man or woman and primitive myths came to be seen in a more favorable light.

During the eighteenth century a tremendous interest in mythology

---

[7]Mayerson, *Myth and Modern Man*, p. 147.

[8]Quoted in *The Rise of Modern Mythology: 1680-1860*, ed. Burton Feldman and Robert D. Richardson (Bloomington: Indiana University Press, 1972), p. 49. Feldman and Richardson have compiled excerpts from dozens of seventeenth-, eighteenth-, and nineteenth-century studies of myth.

arose, but the controversy at the center of all the heightened interest was over the value, rather than the nature, of myth. Rationalists such as Voltaire advocated reason as the arbiter of truth and the guide to understanding; Voltaire dismissed classical mythology (along with the Old and New Testaments) as irrational or as deliberate attempts by the priestly class to mislead humanity. Other no less extreme attacks came from fellow rationalists and deists like Diderot, Volney, and Thomas Paine. According to Robert Richardson, Paine's *The Age of Reason* (Part One, 1794; Part Two, 1796) "did as much as any other single book to fix the terms of the debate between science and mythology and to give the word 'mythology' the connotation of ridiculous falsehood it still bears for many American intellectuals who get their bearings habitually from the Enlightenment."[9]

On the other hand, the Romantic writers of the late eighteenth and early nineteenth centuries regarded poetic myth as a wellspring of human knowledge at least as important as the powers of reason and analysis. At the high point of American Romanticism in the nineteenth century, there existed among American intellectuals a confusing mixture of attitudes about mythology. Bronson Alcott regarded mythology as revealing, in all its forms, the highest religious truths, while his colleague, Theodore Parker, saw it as mere falsehood and superstition, opposed to modern science and historical study.[10] Nevertheless, the major writers of poetry and fiction during the nineteenth century tended to look on mythology as a fountain of inspiration, and many of them drew heavily on classical mythology in their own work. Herman Melville, for instance, found himself turning again and again to figures like Prometheus, Perseus, and Enceladus in order to present an adequate picture of his heroes.[11] Wordsworth lamented the passing of an era in which a vital mythological

---

[9]For a full discussion see Robert D. Richardson, *Mythology and Literature in the American Renaissance* (Bloomington: Indiana University Press, 1978).

[10]Ibid., p. 17.

[11]Two excellent discussions of Melville's use of mythology are Richard Chase, *Herman Melville: A Critical Study* (New York: Macmillan, 1949) and H. Bruce Franklin,

system gave the world a coherency and freshness that it had somehow lost in his own mechanized, skeptical century:

> Great God! I'd rather be a pagan suckled in a creed outworn,
> So might I, standing on this lea,
> Have sights that would make me less forlorn,
> Have glimpse of Proteus rising from the sea,
> Or hear old Triton blow his wreathed horn.

Late in the century, the naughtiest pagan of them all, Algernon Charles Swinburne, wrote a lament for the passing of the old pagan tradition. The lament, "Hymn to Proserpine," takes as a refrain the dying words of the emperor Julian, who was said to have tried to bring back the older, pagan worship and failed, and who grudgingly admitted on his deathbed, "Vicisti, Gallilaee" ("Thou hast conquered, Galilean").[12]

In the twentieth century, interest in mythology has been intensified by the speculations of anthropologists and psychologists, as well as by the more traditional studies of the theologians and literary critics. For Sigmund Freud, myths arose out of man's subconscious, expressing at once both the hopes and the fears that man could deal with in no other manner. Freud's *Totem and Taboo* (1913) carries the subtitle, "Some Points of Agreement Between the Mental Life of Savages and Neurotics." He envisioned a savage act of rebellion in man's prehistory that occasioned the Oedipus myth: one day a band of brothers rebels against a cruel and tyrannical father, a brutal man who had kept all the food and women for himself, driving the younger men away. The brothers kill the father and devour his body, thus taking on some of his strength while they free themselves of his domination. They rejoice in their freedom at first, but inevitably guilt sets in, and they erect taboos against such action and renounce the fruits of their deed—the father's women. Thus arises

---

The Wake of the Gods: Melville's Mythology (Stanford CA: Stanford University Press, 1963).

[12]It might be reasonably argued that Swinburne's poem was merely a cavil against the strictures of Victorian orthodox Christianity and an expression of a desire for what he saw as pagan high-living sensuality.

the Oedipus complex and the only two crimes with which a primitive
society would have to concern itself—parricide and incest.[13] The power
of the Sophoclean tragedy, or modern adaptations of it, depends, says
Freud, not on the conflict between fate and free will, "but upon the
peculiar nature of the material by which this conflict is revealed. There
must be a voice within us that is prepared to acknowledge the compelling
power of fate in Oedipus, while we are able to condemn the situations
occurring in *Die Abnfrau* or other tragedies of fate as arbitrary inventions. . . . His fate moves us only because it might have been our own, because the oracle laid upon us before our birth the very curse that rested
upon him."[14]

Carl Jung took Freud's probings of mythic origins several steps
further. Jung suggested that man is born with an inherited disposition to
behave and think in certain ways. As man has evolved, he has accumu-
lated patterns of thinking. These patterns are handed down to each
succeeding generation, and thus man through the ages receives a larger
and more complex store of memories. The myths of a society express in
elaborate, rather decorative form this storehouse of patterns and racial
memories, but each human mind, even without knowing the specific
myths in detail, shares the predisposition to think in mythic terms. We
share certain primordial shapes or images of thought—in Jung's favorite
term, archetypes. The products of the dreams of normal people or the
visions of neurotic people are seldom fully developed myths, but they
almost always have traceable mythic components. For Jung, mythic
elements (or symbols) were of paramount importance because they
allowed the mind to deal by analogy with that which was as yet unknown
or only in the process of formation. In other words, the mind deals with
the world through the intervention of the archetypes, and when the
archetypes cannot be made to fit a view of the world, chaos ensues. His

---

[13]Later works by Freud which also explore the beginnings of myth are *The Future
of an Illusion* (1927) and *Civilization and its Discontents* (1930).

[14]Quoted in James Burl Hogins, *Literature: Mythology and Folklore* (Chicago:
Science Research Associates, Inc., 1974), p. 37.

conclusion is a powerful case for myth as a producer of order out of chaos: "The mythology of a tribe is its living religion, whose loss is always and everywhere, even in the case of civilized man, a moral catastrophe."[15]

The field of social anthropology has contributed a wealth of ideas to the study of comparative mythology in the last century. The early giant in this area was Sir James George Frazer, who did as much as anyone in the late nineteenth and early twentieth century to arouse popular interest in the subject. Frazer's monumental work, *The Golden Bough* (two volumes in the 1890 edition; eventually expanded to twelve volumes and a supplement), represents the attempt of an English scholar and teacher to stand outside his own culture and examine the beliefs of primitive societies. Having gone through countless editions—some abridged, some illustrated, most bearing prefaces by later mythologists—*The Golden Bough* is still a valuable reference work as well as a classic study in comparative mythology.

Some of Frazer's followers, among them Jane Harrison, championed the view that all myths invariably arose out of the rituals by which gods were propitiated or protection asked. Once the rituals died out of practice, the myths were carried on separately, finding expression later in literature, art, and music.[16] The anthropologist Branislav Malinowski, on the other hand, saw religious ritual as only one facet of the origin of myth in primitive cultures. In a lecture entitled "Myth in Primitive Psychology," Malinowski says that myth is and always has been a way of reinforcing all the standards of a society, and that its most important functions are "in connection with religious ritual, moral influence, and sociological principle."[17] One of the most interesting and controversial of the anthropologi-

---

[15]C. Jung and K. Kerenyi, *Essays on a Science of Mythology* (New York: Pantheon Books, 1949), p. 111. See also Jung, *Collected Papers on a Science of Mythology* (New York: Moffat Yard, 1917).

[16]See especially Harrison's *Themis* (Cambridge: Cambridge University Press, 1912). Other important theorists in the myth-out-of-ritual school are Gilbert Murray, A. B. Cook, F. M. Cornford, and S. H. Hooke.

[17]Reprinted in *Magic, Science, and Religion* (Garden City NY: Doubleday, 1954), p. 98.

cally oriented mythologists is Claude Levi-Strauss. A structural anthropologist, Levi-Strauss uses mythology as a focus to apply his structural method to a study of societies, hoping to provide "a code which is intended to ensure the reciprocal translatability of several myths."[18] He tries, in other words, to discern a number of structural elements that have identical interrelationships in several widely divergent myths from widely divergent cultures.

Some of the most comprehensive attempts (as well as the most readable and most informative) in the twentieth century to bring together various mythic components from widely different cultures are to be found in the works of Joseph Campbell. Campbell's *The Hero With a Thousand Faces* is an effort to distill the essence of the hero in any tradition, to define whatever it is that makes a human being go beyond the bounds of ordinary mortality and so become a mythic hero. Campbell finds a pattern common to all the myths, and he calls this pattern the "monomyth":

> The mythological hero, setting forth from his commonday hut or castle, is lured, carried away, or else voluntarily proceeds, to the threshold of adventure. There he encounters a shadow presence that guards the passage. The hero may defeat or conciliate this power and go alive into the kingdom of the dark (brother-battle, dragon-battle; offering, charm), or be slain by the opponent and descend in death (dismemberment, crucifixion). Beyond the threshold, then, the hero journeys through a world of unfamiliar yet strangely intimate forces, some of which severely threaten him (tests), some of which give magical aid (helpers). When he arrives at the nadir of the mythological round, he undergoes a supreme ordeal and gains his reward. The triumph may be represented as the hero's sexual union with the goddess-mother of the world (sacred marriage), his recognition by the father-creator (father atonement), his own divinization (apotheosis), or again—if the powers have remained unfriendly to him— his theft of the boon he came to gain (bride-theft, fire-theft); intrinsically it is an expression of consciousness and therewith of being (illumination,

[18]Claude Levi-Strauss, *The Raw and the Cooked: Introduction to a Science of Mythology*, trans. John and Doreen Weightman, 1 (New York: Harper and Row, 1969), p. 5.

transfiguration, freedom). The final work is that of the return. If the powers have blessed the hero, he now sets forth under their protection (emissary); if not, he flees and is pursued (transformation flight, obstacle flight). At the return threshold the transcendental powers must remain behind; the hero re-emerges from the kingdom of dread (return, resurrection). The boon that he brings restores the world (elixir).[19]

Thus all myths of the hero are, in a sense, the same myth since they share common elements. Myths arise just as dreams arise, Campbell says, in man's subconscious mind which deals with hopes and fears that have scarcely been articulated.

In concluding this chapter, I should like to return to the observation of Carl Jung that I quoted earlier: "The mythology of a tribe is its living religion, whose loss is always and everywhere, even in the case of civilized man, a moral catastrophe." Man uses myths, in one form or another, to think about his world—in order to give direction and coherency to his world. To a very large extent, the mythology of a civilization (or of a nation, or an individual) both shapes and is shaped by a particular view of the world. J.R.R. Tolkien once wrote a wonderful essay on the poem *Beowulf* in which he dealt with the essential difference between the Northern mythological tradition and the tradition of Greece and Rome. The Northern view is darker—is, in fact, catastrophic—for in Norse mythology even the gods must die. There will come a time when gods and men together will go down in battle against the forces of darkness and chaos. This is *ragnarok*, the death of everything, the end of order, the twilight of the gods (*Gotterdammerung*). Yet somehow this defeat is no refutation: the struggle itself, even ending as it must in death, is sufficient affirmation.

There is nothing like this in Greek or Roman mythology, nothing at all, and perhaps that is why readers who are used to the Southern tradition might find works like *Beowulf* or the *Volsungasaga* or the *Eddas*

---

[19]*The Hero With a Thousand Faces* (Princeton: Princeton University Press, 1968), pp. 245-46. See also Campbell's four-volume work, *The Masks of God* (New York: The Viking Press, 1969). A much briefer but still useful study of the hero is David Adams Leeming, *Mythology: The Voyage of the Hero* (New York: Harper and Row, 1981).

curious or confusing. The Southern tradition, says Tolkien, "may hold
the promise of a profounder thought. In any case it was a virtue of the
Southern mythology that it could not stop where it was. It must go
forward to philosophy or relapse into anarchy."[20] But the Northern
imagination made the darkness immortal, made the monsters immortal,
"put the monsters in the centre, gave them victory but no honour, and
found a potent but terrible solution in naked will and courage." The poem
presents a series of tableaus, says Tolkien, and each one of them suggests
the Northern mythological view of man's fate in the world and his
relation to it. "At the beginning, and during the poem's process, and most
of all at the end, we look down as if from a visionary height upon the
house of man in the valley of the world. A light starts—*lixte se leoma ofer
landa fela* [its radiance gleamed over many lands]—and there is a sound
of music; but the outer darkness and its hostile offspring lie ever in wait
for the torches to fail and the voices to cease. Grendel is maddened by the
sound of harps."[21] One simply cannot imagine a work like *Beowulf* being
produced by a poet like Homer or Hesiod or any other Southern writer. It
is a distinctly Northern work, however much its composer may have
been influenced by exposure to other traditions, including the
Christian.[22]

Every college student who has ever taken a course in biblical
literature knows that the flood story in Genesis is a very old tale that
recurs, with some variation, throughout the Mideast. (Many societies

---

[20]Lewis E. Nicholson, ed., "Beowulf: The Monsters and the Critics," *An Anthology of Beowulf Criticism,* (Notre Dame: University of Notre Dame Press, 1963), p. 77.

[21]Ibid., p. 88. The description is reminiscent of Bede's famous analogy of man's life to the flight of a bird leaving a vast, stormy darkness, entering a warm, lighted hall, and departing again into the storm. Notice also the frequent descriptions of Grendel as a lonely figure who lives on the edge of the world of light and order. He is a *mearcstapa* (borderland walker), an *angengea* (solitary journeyer), and a *sceadugengea* (walker in darkness).

[22]*Beowulf* was probably composed in England around 735, well over a century after the coming of St. Augustine to the island. The mixture of Northern and Christian ideals is nowhere more evident than in the conclusion, where Beowulf is lamented as "The kindest of worldly kings/Mildest, most gentle, most eager for fame."

from all over the world have a flood story. The pervasiveness of the tale
may be due to the origins of so many early civilizations along major
waterways: the Indus, the Tigris-Euphrates, the Nile.) One of the flood
stories that is especially close in some of its details to the Genesis account
is a section from *The Epic of Gilgamesh*. The epic itself is a secular tale about
a hero's attempt to learn the secret of immortality. Dating back to perhaps
the beginning of the second millenium, B.C., the poem offers a version of
the flood story that in some ways is remarkably close to the biblical story
of Noah and the ark. The ancient Akkadian or Babylonian version of
Noah, a man named Utnapishtim, is instructed by the gods to tear down
his house, give up his worldly possessions, build a ship, and take aboard it
"the seed of all living things." Utnapishtim tells Gilgamesh that he obeyed
the gods, built a ship, and floated around in it with his family and the seed
of all living things until the waters began to recede. When the ship came
to rest on a mountain, he sent out first a dove, then a swallow, and finally
a raven to check for the existence of dry land. (Compare the account in
Genesis 8.) When the raven did not come back, Utnapishtim offered
sacrifices to the gods—all except the god Enlil, who had brought on the
flood:

> Let the gods come to the offering;
> But let not Enlil come to the offering,
> For he, unreasoning, brought on the deluge
> And my people consigned to destruction.[23]

The key word here is "unreasoning." It did not occur to the
composer of the poem to fix a reason for the god's action; Enlil and the
other gods decided to drown the world, so they did. There was no reason
for Utnapishtim's being saved. He was not any more righteous than
anybody else, at least as far as we can discern from the text. He just
happened to get saved and everybody else just happened to get drowned.

---

[23]*The Epic of Gilgamesh*, 11, p. 167-69, in *The Ancient Near East: An Anthology of Texts and Pictures*, ed. James B. Pritchard (Princeton: Princeton University Press, 1958), p. 70.

This is a very non-Western way of looking at the world. The Hebrews drew much of their own tradition from sources common to the Summerians, Akkadians, and Hittites—and came up with a version of the story that is similar in detail but remarkably different in outlook. The Hebrew version suggests in the first place a belief in a concerned and rational deity, but more important it suggests an interest in cause-and-effect thinking. Something has happened and here are the reasons. Mankind was wicked, so God decided to destroy the whole race; because Noah wasn't too bad, God decided to save him and his family and to use him as an instrument for rebuilding human life on earth. Western readers find the Genesis account palatable not only because of a belief in a concerned deity, but also because the story makes sense to a mind that is conditioned to see cause-and-effect in all phenomena. Our inheritance, after all, is not only Hebrew but Greek as well. Like Aristotle, we look for reason, for causes—we are scientific. The East, whatever wonderful things it accomplished in other fields, never produced anything resembling science; it did not concern itself, as our tradition did, with the overwhelming question, "Why?" The Genesis account of the flood is Western in its mythic outlook. The Akkadian account, so remarkably similar in some of its details, is Eastern in outlook, and interesting as it may be for its own sake, seems to the Western mind quaint, incomplete, and perplexing.[24]

Mythology is, in a very real sense, a language. It allows the user to deal with phenomena in relation to a framework or background of tales. It puts new experiences into a familiar context much as a language does. A man who had never seen a bulldog before would nonetheless recognize the first one he saw as a dog and would fit it immediately into a

---

[24]The most perplexing (in this sense) book in the Old Testament is the Book of Job, and for precisely the same reason. Job learns there sometimes aren't any reasons at all for the terrible or the wonderful things in human existence; they just happen. "Why" is an irrelevant question. Most biblical scholars agree that the ending of the Book of Job is an emendation, doubtless tacked on generations —perhaps centuries— later by someone unwilling or unable to accept the worldview presented in the first part of the book.

convenient frame of reference. On the other hand, a man from the tropics who had no knowledge, either direct or indirect, of winter might be utterly confused by his first glimpse of snow. Because nothing in his background would have prepared him for what he would see and touch, he would surely feel lost and amazed—literally beyond words, for no words he knew would fit his experience.

Anyone doubting this has only to watch a small child's reaction to his first sight and feel of the ocean. At first there is the confused and hurried reaching for words, as one would reach for stones or melons to find just the right one: water, big, moving, noise, sand, bright. "It's the ocean," some adult says. "Ocean," the child repeats, and suddenly he has a key by which he will come to comprehend not only the whole Atlantic, but all seas everywhere. The key is only a word.

If language were to break down, man would be suddenly at a loss for a way to comprehend the world, for language is not just a way of communicating with others but a way of ordering our experience of the world. Since the human mind is such an inventive and elastic thing, the complete breakdown of a language is unlikely. The breakdown of a mythology, on the other hand, is a distinct possibility in any age, and its consequences, while not so dire as the consequences of a loss of language, are still serious. When a mythological tradition is no longer vital, when people in a society no longer believe in or take seriously the stories and the heroes that make up the tradition, then the society may be threatened by chaos.

Just as the mind of the child reaches for words to describe the ocean, rejecting each one as inadequate, so the society that has outgrown or outlived its mythic tradition searches for a new way to make sense of the world. Throughout history, changes in the mythic structure of a society have been accompanied by outbreaks of violence and creativity as people reacted to the uncertainties of change and tried to create new ways of seeing the world. Consider the enormous changes in the way man visualized the world that were brought about by advances in science and by the geographical discoveries of the fifteenth, sixteenth, and seventeenth centuries. Some of these advances and discoveries played havoc with the perfect order portrayed by the extant mythological structures of the time because they necessitated a new way of observing the world. The records of the day tell us that it was a confusing and an exciting time; we call the burst of creativity that accompanied the confusion the Renaissance.

The collapse of the geocentric world view was surely the most disturbing change of the late Renaissance, since the collapse implied that man did not, after all, occupy stage center in creation. It is no accident, I think, that some of the most creative thinkers of the period were engaged in balancing two visions of the universe that were absolutely irreconcilable. John Donne observed that the "new philosophy called all in doubt," but out of that doubt came a complex and restless poetic genius. Milton's images of the universe come from a world view he could neither quite believe nor abandon—the view that was Ptolemy's. Perhaps the effort to sustain in the mind one world view (or one mythic system) while reaching for another helps to produce a *Paradise Lost*. At any rate, some of the most productive periods of history have come during times when mythic structures which had once proved satisfactory were being discarded and new ones were taking their places. No doubt this is because the collapse of a mythology threatens to turn coherency into chaos, and it takes a tremendous creative effort to salvage whatever is salvageable and forge ahead to make a new order. Hemingway, Pound, Fitzgerald, Faulkner, Eliot, Sartre, and Camus all began their writing careers at about the time people began to talk about "post-war disillusionment." Disillusionment meant essentially the loss of a coherent system—or a large part of it—and out of that disillusionment came the most literary excitement and some of the best thinking this century has produced so far.

We reach for order through myth. When our myths have to be abandoned because they no longer work for us, we reach for new myths. The perplexity and confusion of the modern world, its seeming lack of coherency, the pervasive sense of isolation that is so often a theme in our literature (and in our lives) are all results of our position between myths.

We have let go of some traditions, we are reaching for others (or, in some cases, making a rather desperate grab back for the old ones), and we feel ourselves floating, in a sense—not quite belonging, as we believe our predecessors somehow belonged, to anything very stable. Joseph Campbell has said that through mythology man touches something immortal, something beyond the merely human and transient, and so feels himself a part of a coherent world: "For those in whom a local mythology still works, there is an experience both of accord with the social order, and of harmony with the universe. For those, however, in whom the authorized signs no longer work, . . . there follows inevitably a sense both of dissociation from the local social nexus and of quest, within and without, for life, which the brain will take to be for 'meaning.' "[25] It is our own peculiar position to have been virtually awash for several generations in a bewildering array of traditions, from charismatic Christianity to a secular millenarianism to Maoism to psychoanalysis, and to have been able to embrace none of them. We are not mythless, but our mythology often seems inconsistent and confusing, and our view of order is elusive.

---

[25] *The Masks of God: Creative Mythology* (New York: The Viking Press, 1975), p. 5.

Chapter 2

The Breakup
of Systems

*L'eternel silence de ces
espaces infinis m'effraie.*
—BLAISE PASCAL

ONE OF THE MOST melancholy documents of the last three and a half centuries is the confession of Galileo, signed in Rome on 22 June 1633. It is melancholy because it suggests the desperate measures that any society or group will go to in order to protect its own, peculiar mythic interpretation of the world, even if those measures include torture and murder. The confession begins, "I, Galileo Galilei, son of the late Vincenzo Galilei, Florentine, aged seventy years, arraigned personally before this tribunal, and kneeling before you, most Eminent and Reverend Lord Cardinals, Inquisitors general against heretical depravity throughout the whole Christian Republic, having before my eyes and touching with my hands the holy Gospels—swear that I have always believed, do now believe, and by God's help will for the future believe, all that is held, preached, and taught by the Holy Catholic and Apostolic Roman Church." It goes on to spell out his sin: that he "wrote and printed a book" in which he discussed (not defended, not championed, but *discussed*) "the false opinion that the sun is the centre of the world and immovable, and that the earth is not the centre of the world, and moves." It ends with the solemn, "I, Galileo Galilei, have abjured as above with my own hand."[1]

Galileo lived in an exciting age of exploration and discovery. He was born in Italy in 1564—the same year, incidentally, that Shakespeare was born in England and nine years after Copernicus had published his momentous book, *De Revolutionibus Orbium Coelestium (The Revolution of the Heavenly Orbs)*. The whole world was in intellectual upheaval during Galileo's life; in particular, the new concept of a heliocentric universe was exciting and perplexing scientists, philosophers, and churchmen alike. The Catholic Church felt itself challenged on several fronts and had begun, in reaction to these challenges, to assert its authority with vehemence. The challenges were real enough. England was by now thoroughly lost to Protestantism; Luther had long since struck a serious blow against Catholic power all over Northern Europe, and other reformers had followed him. In 1618 the Thirty Years War, pitting Protestant against Catholic, began. But perhaps the most dangerous attempt against the authority of the church was—or at least seemed to be—the Copernican theory of the universe.

Nicolas Copernicus died before the church could attack him directly for his controversial theory; his book appeared only days before his death. But the church did its best to see that the theory was not spread because Copernicanism seemed to go against the very basis of Christian mythology.

The medieval world, the universe of Ptolemy, was an orderly and coherent place—or at least the Ptolemaic model of it was orderly and coherent. It presented, as Arthur O. Lovejoy has pointed out, a world that "was definitely limited and fenced about," making the world "pictur- able." It was not small, but it did not baffle the imagination with its

---

[1]Among the excellent brief discussions of the circumstances surrounding Gali- leo's trial is Israel Shenker, "After 340 Years, Galileo May Beat the Inquisition," *Smithsonian* 12 (August 1981): 90-96. See also Jacob Bronowski, *The Ascent of Man* (Boston: Little, Brown, and Company), pp. 194-218. I use the translation of Galileo's confession in Bronowski, pp. 216-17.

endlessness. Medieval men and women lived in a walled universe just as they lived in walled towns. The theory of Copernicus threatened to break down the walls.[2]

In the Ptolemaic view, the earth lay at the very center of the universe and around the earth moved, in a stately and predictable procession, the seven planets—including, of course, the sun. They ran in perfect circles and around those circles within circles lay a ring of fixed stars. It was an acceptable and workable model of the universe for two reasons—the same reasons that any model is acceptable and workable in any age. In the first place, the model agreed with observable phenomena. After all, the sun appears to rise in the east and set in the west—our very language still reflects this geocentric view of the universe. The heavens do appear to surround us like a starry cap or bowl; and if we assume that the world is round, we must then assume that the bowl is a complete sphere or set of spheres. Astronomical observances coincided, for the most part, with the model. (The ancient Phoenicians, long before Ptolemy, knew all there was to know about navigating a boat by the positions of the stars. That the stars were not, in their view of the world, quite what they are in ours made no practical differences at all.) Mathematics—in the final analysis, probably the best hope of any scientific civilization for understanding its own models—worked smoothly under the system until more sophisticated methods of observation in the early Renaissance suggested the need for a new kind of mathematics.[3]

But just as important was the fact that the model reinforced and

---

[2]Arthur O. Lovejoy, *The Great Chain of Being: A Study of the History of an Idea* (New York: Harper and Row, 1965), p. 101.

[3]Discoveries around the year 1600 led Johannes Kepler to conclude that the movements of the planets were not regular in speed and circular in pattern, but irregular and elliptical. This in itself was a disturbing conclusion, for it called into question the notion that the heavens were designed on that self-evident image of perfection in nature, the circle or sphere. Even more disturbing was the fact that the mathematics of the day could by no means account for the irregularities in motion and shape, and remained unable to do so until the invention of the differential calculus later in the seventeenth century.

supported the dominant myths of the period. Traditional Christianity was married to the Ptolemaic view of the universe because the model invented by Ptolemy in Alexandria around 150 A.D. made credible, even probable, the truth of the entire mythic system on which Christianity was based. To the contemporaries of Copernicus, the geocentric model made sense because it demonstrated the importance of the earth in God's scheme of things.

Ptolemy's science made the prescientific creation myth in Genesis perfectly plausible. It made a three-storied universe, such as the one Milton pictured much later in *Paradise Lost* with heaven at the top, the created world (the earth and its various encircling spheres) in the middle, and hell at the bottom— not only a theological and mythical pattern but a logical one as well. If God had wanted to stop the motion of the sun across the sky so as to lengthen a day of battle, such a feat would certainly have been possible under the Ptolemaic scheme. Finally, since man was the capstone of creation, the final effort, the one creature in whom God took special pride or delight and who alone could cause God to be displeased, it was fitting that man occupy stage center, surrounded by all the lesser elements of creation as a great performer might be surrounded by lesser actors on a stage.[4]

The Pope and the cardinals in Galileo's time were convinced of the necessity to stop the teaching of the heliocentric world view and to undermine by any means whatsoever the credibility of those scientists who dared to teach it, because the new notion seemed to them to threaten the very basis of their mythological system. And they were quite right; it did pose just such a threat, although the full effects of that threat were not to be realized for several more centuries. One duty of the Inquisition was

---

[4]Lovejoy argues convincingly that in the strictly orthodox scheme of things inherited from Ptolemy, man's position was actually as far removed as possible from God, and the Ptolemaic cosmology thus "served rather for man's humiliation than his exaltation" (*Great Chain of Being* p. 102). He concedes, however, that the older view, "however low the place it assigned to man in his unregenerate state, at all events attributed a unique significance to terrestial history.... The Universe was at least not a many-ringed circus" (p. 143).

to smell out anything that smacked of Copernicanism and to deal with it in such a way that no doubt would remain as to the power and authority of the church. By 1616, the Holy Office had suppressed the work of Copernicus, condemned the attempt of a Carmelite friar named Paolo Foscarini to reconcile Copernicanism and Christianity, ordered Galileo to abstain from teaching the new doctrine, and burned to death the philosopher, Giordano Bruno.[5]

Galileo waited until after the death of Pope Paul V to again present the ideas of Copernicus in any form. Even then, he proceeded cautiously at first. He came to Rome in 1624 and had several conferences with Paul V's successor, an intellectual and patron of the arts named Maffeo Barberini, Pope Urban VIII. However, the new pope was not much more pleased with heliocentrism than the old one had been. Galileo did not publish his *Dialogues on the Two Chief World Systems* until 1632, and then only after declaring the whole work to have been a "poetical conceit," and qualifying his theories as "dreams, nullities, paralogisms, and chimeras." On 1 October of that year, he received a summons to appear in Rome within thirty days to answer to the Inquisition.[6]

Between April and June of 1633, Galileo was interrogated three times by the cardinals and officers of the Inquisition. He was seventy then and in poor health. By the end of his trial, he was dangerously weak and nearly broken in spirit. The Pope directed that Galileo be shown the instruments of torture, including the rack, and that he be threatened with torture. Furthermore, he was to be imprisoned and was to be forbidden even to discuss the theories of Copernicus on pain of torture and death. He lived for nine more years, a prisoner in his own house at Arcetri, near Florence, a victim of the blind hatred and fear aroused by his inadvertent attack on the mythology of the day.

---

[5]Bruno expanded the theory of Copernicus to envision a completely decentralized and infinite universe—a vast and threatening cosmology indeed. He traveled all over Europe discussing the idea that man is not unique in the universe. He refused to abjure his beliefs, and the Inquisition killed him in 1600.

[6]Shenker, "Galileo May Beat the Inquisition," p. 94.

The case of Galileo may seem extreme, but it is not without parallels. Any thinker or reformer in any age who places or seems to place under attack the dominant mythic structure of the age can expect harsh treatment. Such people are not mere annoyances; they are threats, dangerous adversaries of the very order that makes life coherent and meaningful. It was Galileo's (and Bruno's) lot to have been perceived correctly—as a threat to a system of order that was already beginning to lose its power, and realizing this, had to hold on to that power even more desperately and viciously than before.

By the end of the sixteenth century, as E. M. W. Tillyard has pointed out, the medieval world view was precarious, but the new order was still terrifyingly disorderly.[7] It is interesting, by the way, to note the depths of dismay attendant on the death of Elizabeth I in 1603. Englishmen under Elizabeth had felt themselves to be riding the crest of a wave; the wildly extravagant compliments, in Spenser and elsewhere, to the queen and the order her reign represented were not mere effusions designed to ingratiate the poets. They were sincere—if sometimes flowery, to our tastes—expressions of the delight and wonder Elizabethans felt at being a part of the order that the queen's reign seemed to represent. For a time, at least, chaos was held at bay. As Elizabeth grew older and the ascendancy of James of Scotland grew more apparent, there were increased expressions of concern about that perfect order. When, in the first few years of James I's reign, the plague broke out, fire destroyed much of London, and Guy Fawkes tried to blow up Parliament, Englishmen felt order crumbling around them. (Some scholars believe that the Jacobean tragedies of Shakespeare reflect precisely this concern. Perhaps for those who watched *Othello*, as well as for the Moor himself, "chaos [had] come againe.") At any rate, the last thing that Elizabethans wanted or needed

---

[7]Tillyard says that the Elizabethans "were terrified lest order should be upset, and appalled by the visible tokens of disorder that suggested its upsetting. They were obsessed by the fear of chaos and the fact of mutability; and the obsession was powerful in proportion as their faith in cosmic order was strong." *The Elizabethan World Picture* (New York: Vintage Books, 1960), p. 16.

was a demonstration, such as that provided by Giordano Bruno when he visited Oxford, that the universe is really a rather untidy place.

What the scientists of the sixteenth and early seventeenth centuries said was simply this: the old way of viewing man's relationship to the rest of the universe no longer agrees with observable phenomena. It is, in that sense, no longer true. The scientists were resisted and, in some cases, persecuted because representatives of the dominant mythic system realized that if the old way of looking at the world were no longer true, then the myths that depended to a very great extent on that world view could also be called into question. The destruction of the basis of a mythic system was nothing less than the destruction of order itself; the threat was real and immediate. It is possible, in fact, to simplify the struggle of the church in the West to maintain its traditional mythology in the face of contradictory evidence as a series of battles beginning around 1600, reaching a fever pitch in the nineteenth century, and continuing to the present day. This is by no means because men like Copernicus or Galileo in the sixteenth century—or Charles Darwin in the nineteenth—set out to attack established religion. It is instead because their theories about the world called into question many of the tales that were, from their inception, demonstrations of another order, another view of the world entirely.

It is not necessary in a book of this sort to examine in detail the furor surrounding the publication of Darwin's *The Origin of Species* in 1859 or *The Descent of Man* a few years later. It is important for twentieth-century observers to realize that Darwin, like Galileo, was a target of the aroused people within the dominant mythic system who were threatened or seemingly threatened by his theories. He was assuredly not either the first or only theorist whose work had disturbed Victorians, but his name came to be associated, long after 1859, with the science-versus-revealed-religion controversy in the nineteenth century, as if he had started it all almost singlehandedly. In fact, Victorians in general were fascinated by science more so than any previous generation had been. The Crystal Palace exhibit in 1851 was a monument not only to technology but to scientific progress and speculation as well. One might say that nineteenth-century man was rapidly building an alternate mythic system, based generally on the idea of man's ultimate perfectibility through scientific and technological progress, before Darwin ever published anything. It is, I believe, quite proper to see the Crystal Palace as a kind of Victorian Parthenon, in which were housed, like pentellic marble statues, the tangible symbols and forms of the intangible gods, technology and science.

The geologist Lyell had caught the imagination of students and intellectuals in the 1830s with his discoveries of fossils, and his work had done much to upset established theories about the age of the earth. Finding oneself suddenly in an unthinkably old universe has much the same effect as finding oneself suddenly in an unthinkably large one; a feeling of loss of orderly progression and definition may follow. It was not that most people accepted as true Bishop Usher's estimate of the date of creation (4,004, B.C.—derived, I assume, by counting back the "begats" in the Book of Genesis), but the geological finds of the day pointed to a vast, generative "process" occupying untold millions of years. Entire species had developed, flourished for ages, then died out, to be replaced by others that would do the same. Years before Darwin, some dared think—and speak—the unthinkable, that even man was a part of this eyeless, mindless process, and hence no different, in essence, from any other part of nature.

This is precisely the fear that Tennyson voices in the most agonizing (and, in many ways, the most effective) sections of *In Memoriam* (1850). The speaker in the poem wants to trust

> That nothing walks with aimless feet;
> That not one life shall be destroyed,
> Or cast as rubbish to the void,
> When God hath made the pile complete.

Looking around him, though, he realizes that he can find no evidence for a belief in any such benevolent plan. His faith seems dreamlike and his creed that of "an infant crying in the night; / An infant crying for the light; / And with no language but a cry." If he cannot trust in the existence of a divine plan encompassing every individual, every "sparrow that falls," perhaps he can count on the design of God for the human race in general. He calls it "the larger hope," but Lyell's discoveries seem to repudiate even this:

"So careful of the type?" but no.
From scarped cliff and quarried stone
She [Nature] cries, "A thousand types are gone;
I care for nothing, all shall go."

This is the empty universe, the godless universe without will or purpose that we see so clearly in the work of Hemingway, Camus, Sartre, and other modern writers. It is a world in which the old tales have lost their truth and their meaning, so the world has lost its order. Tennyson worked his way out of this vision, depending finally on a kind of faith that could not be assailed by mere scientific observation. Much earlier, Pascal had also had to depend on faith alone to get him over the nightmarish void that the Copernican universe had opened to him. He saw the void, though, and he recognized its threat to his system of order: "The eternal silence of these infinite spaces terrifies me."

The traditional religious world view in the nineteenth century was jeopardized not only by the evidence provided by the scientific community, but by the tendency in biblical studies called "higher criticism." Beginning in Germany under the leadership of scholars like D. F. Strauss, higher criticism purported to examine the Bible in exactly the same way and using the same criteria that would be used to examine any other text. The result was an interesting inversion of the seventeenth-century tendency to find traces of sacred (read "Christian") truth in tales from other mythic traditions. To the consternation of religious conservatives all over Europe, Strauss and his colleagues began to study the biblical tales as if they were in no essential way different from the tales of other traditions.

It was a perfectly logical and natural development in an age of science and investigation. In a very real sense, it was the natural legacy of Copernicus and other astronomers and the philosophers of the sixteenth and seventeenth centuries, because once the basic concept of man's relationship to the rest of the universe had changed (most notably, his ideas about its size, shape, age, and even its ordering), the tales that reflected and demonstrated the older ideas were open to logical investigation in light of the new concepts of order. Once that door was opened, speculation on the myths of the Judeo-Christian tradition became rampant. It was easy to point out, for instance, that numerous mythic traditions have tales about a virgin birth, a sacrificial figure whose death regenerates or spiritually renews his people, and a demigod who was born, suffered, died as a man, and was then given new life. Clearly, the study of comparative mythology had reached a new and exciting level of sophistication, but the results were unnerving to many people in the mainstream of traditional religion.

One interesting effort to revitalize Christianity in the face of the loss of its mythic power was Rudolf Bultmann's "demythifying" of the Bible. Realizing that with the collapse of the "three-storied" universe, many of the tales of the Bible seemed to alienate rather than excite or attract modern readers, Bultmann sought to purge the tradition of what seemed its more fanciful elements, bringing it more into line with modern thinking. Whether a traditional mythic system can exist devoid of its own myths, however, would seem to be a question of semantics.

Robert Browning has a fascinating poem about the loss of myth, or of the power of myth, in the late nineteenth century. The poem, "Bishop Blougram's Apology," is often interpreted as Browning's rather sardonic portrayal of a worldly, sophisticated, and thoroughly hypocritical bishop.[8] It is not. The central issue in the poem is not hypocrisy but mythology—the role of mythology in creating order in the face of chaos. In a monologue to a nonbeliever, a young journalist named Gigadibs, the bishop offers an unusual defense for the retention of a coherent mythic

---

[8]See, for instance, F. Hillis Miller, *The Disappearance of God: Five Nineteenth-Century Writers* (Cambridge: The Belknap Press, 1963). Miller links Blougram with the charlatan Mr. Sludge and the diabolic Guido Francescini, calling the three "examples of grotesque and funguslike excresence, deviation, idiosyncracy." See also G. K. Chesterton, *Robert Browning* (London: MacMillan, 1903), and Robert Langbaum, *The Poetry of Experience* (New York: W.W. Norton, 1963).

system, even though events seem to make belief in the individual myths impossible.

Blougram begins, oddly enough, by pointing to the obvious material advantages his position as bishop affords him. There is an air of almost vulgar opulence in his casual references to good wine, good books, luxury, and power. He seems proud of his seat in the church and anxious to justify his faith because it has, after all, been very lucrative. If we assume that the bishop argues this way because it is the only way he knows how to argue, then surely we must find him as hypocritical as Gigadibs had accused. But Browning's own statement that the poem was in no way a satire on Cardinal Wiseman or on Catholicism in general is hard to reconcile with this assumption. Blougram realizes that Gigadibs would never accept any argument which started out on spiritual, otherworldly grounds—to begin his defense of faith in this manner would only invite a superior, cynical sneer from his opponent. Gigadibs must have at least a nodding acquaintance with higher criticism and probably is aware of the recent controversy over the authorship and authenticity of the Gospel of John. He has come to this meeting prepared to disparage the very ground on which he supposes Blougram must make his defense. Therefore, the bishop chooses to meet Gigadibs first on the young man's own ground; he says simply that faith is a great deal more lucrative than nonfaith.

Such a statement would be foolish indeed in the presence of a believer, but as Gigadibs has already accused the bishop of being too otherworldly for a man of good sense, he certainly cannot accuse him of being too worldly as well. Reluctantly, he is forced to admit that, if material values are the only real values in life, Bishop Blougram leads a very fine life. Using the same Gigadibsian premise—that earthly goals are the only real ones—Blougram indicates that he is a much more successful man than, say, William Shakespeare:

> Did Shakespeare live, he could but sit at home
> And get himself in dreams the Vatican,
> Greek busts, Venetian paintings, Roman walls,
> And English books, none equal to his own,
> Which I read, bound in gold (he never did).

The patient bishop moves Gigadibs from point to point with insulting ease, a superb logician manipulating a fairly simple thinker, until the journalist is forced to admit that his own basic premise is absurd. Once "back on Christian ground," as the bishop says (back to the premise that there is more to life than merely the accumulation of wealth and luxury), Blougram begins the process of building a defense for his religion. He grants that faith cannot be certain; there can be no sure knowledge, no empirical proof. A desire to believe, however, is "faith enough":

> It is the idea, the feeling and the love,
> God means mankind should strive for and show faith
> Whatever be the process to that end—
> And not historic knowledge, logic sound,
> And metaphysical acumen, sure!

Blougram's first step was to discredit the idea that material values were the only real values. That done, he proceeded to establish the notion of a need for faith, even when the faith cannot be believed in as strictly as one believes "in fire that it will burn." He is now ready to defend what has seemed to Gigadibs indefensible, a belief in the myths of the Bible, including the miracles and divinity of Christ. His defense rests ultimately on the insistence that only through a belief in something tangible—a god who became man, for instance—can man have a religion that is at all meaningful. The miracles Gigadibs has scorned are important as tangible ways in which the divine is involved with the human; to discard belief in the simplest one of them is to open the way for doubts about the rest. Eventually, religion becomes meaningless, and God remains only as an idea in the mind of man:

> I hear you recommend, I might at least
> Eliminate, decrassify my faith
> Since I adopt it; keeping what I must   .
> And leaving what I can—such points as this.
> I won't—that is, I can't throw one away.
>   . . . . .
> To such a process I discern no end.
> Clearing off one excrescence to see two,
> There's ever a next in size, now grown as big,

That meets the knife; I cut and cut again!
First comes the Liquefication, what comes last
But Fichte's clever cut at God himself?

The whole body of Judeo-Christian mythology, complete with its
wild illogicalities, its inconsistencies, its man-god and its miracles, is, for
the bishop, the means by which man can approach an understanding of
the very concept of God.[9] Direct knowledge of the deity is impossible;
man's mind could not stand such a revelation:

Naked belief in God the Omnipotent
Omniscient, Omnipresent, sears too much
The sense of conscious creatures to be borne.
          . . . . .
Under a vertical sun, the exposed brain
And lidless eye and disimprisoned heart
Less certainly would wither up at once
Than mind, confronted with the truth of Him.

If the miracles did not exist as historical facts, then, they would have to be
made up and believed anyway. Religion without an attendant mythology
is impossible, Blougram says, and the myths are to be taken very seriously.
The knife of skepticism which trims away first a belief in the least tenable
of the stories must later cut into the belief in a god who is concerned with
human affairs, and ultimately will destroy any belief in a god whatsoever.
Blougram sees man's countless sciences

                    . . . cosmogony,
Geology, ethnology, what not,
(Greek endings, each the little passing-bell
That signifies some faith's about to die),

---

[9]C. R. Tracy notes that in "Ferishtah's Fancies" and the *Parleyings*, Browning
"argues for the validity of an anthropomorphic faith against the cavils of objectors like
Herbert Spencer." Tracy also says that the monster Caliban approaches an understanding of a non-anthropomorphic god ("the quiet") only through a belief in a god created
in his own image (Setebos). See "Caliban upon Setebos," *Studies in Philology*, 35 (April
1938): 491. See also W. O. Raymond, "Browning and Higher Criticism" *PMLA*, 44
(December, 1929): 590-621.

as the outgrowth of the wish to explain away all the mysteries of the universe empirically. But Sylvester Blougram, who (Browning says) "believed, say, half he spoke," suggests that empiricism alone cannot provide the kinds of answers man seeks. It can tell him about quantity and degree, but not about meaning. Only myth does that.

When myths die, gods die. And when gods die, the civilizations which had originally raised them up for worship can see themselves as threatened by an immense void, an emptiness. The empty, staring blankness of the godless universe offers man a new and terrifying kind of freedom: the freedom to choose among things which have no value. One can do no better here than to quote at length from Nietzsche, who first and most powerfully presented the death of God. In Nietzsche's story, a madman with a lantern appears in the market place in the early morning, and he shouts to tell the people the news of the disappearance of God:

> "Whither is God," he cried. "I shall tell you. *We have killed him*— you and I. All of us are his murderers. But how have we done this? How were we able to drink up the sea? Who gave us the sponge to wipe away the entire horizon? What did we do when we unchained this earth from its sun? Whither is it moving now? Whither are we moving now? Away from all suns? Are we not plunging continually? Backward, sideward, forward, in all directions? Is there any up or down left? Are we not straying as through an infinite nothing? Do we not feel the breath of empty space? Has it not become colder? Is not night and more night coming on all the while? Must not lanterns be lit in the morning? Do we not hear anything yet of the noise of the grave-diggers who are burying God? Do we not smell anything yet of God's decomposition? Gods too decompose. God is dead. God remains dead. And we have killed him. . . . Who will wipe this blood off us? What water is there for us to cleanse ourselves? . . . Is not the greatness of this deed too great for us? Must we not ourselves become gods simply to seem worthy of it?"
>
> Here the madman fell silent and looked again at his listeners; and they too were silent and stared at him in astonishment. At last he threw the lantern on the ground, and it broke and went out. "I come too early," he said then. "My time has not come yet. . . . Lightning and thunder require time, the light of stars requires time, deeds require time even after they are done, before they can be seen and heard. This deed is still more distant from them than the most distant stars—and yet they have done it themselves."

> It has been related further that on that same day the madman entered divers churches and there sang his *requiem aeternum deo*. Led out and called to account, he is said to have replied each time, "What are these churches now if they are not the tombs and sepulchres of God?"

Nietzsche here anticipates the anguish, the despair, that we often associate with the writings of the major existentialists like Jaspers, Heidegger, and Sartre; he also predicts here that the spectre haunting future generations will be the spectre of nihilism, a complete loss of meaning. ("Is there any up or down left?") In other works, especially in *The Will to Power*, Nietzsche suggests that the only thing modern man will be able to find that will replace his dead god is the mere accumulation of power, in one form or another. In the face of the loss of all supernal values, the only value left is power—absolute control over others and over one's own environment. This is the only goal of a nihilistic society, and William Barrett finds it a hauntingly accurate portrayal of twentieth-century America. "Despite all its apparently cheerful and self-satisfied immersion in gadgets and refrigerators," Barrett says, "American life, one suspects, is nihilistic to its core. Its final 'What for?' is not even asked, let alone answered."[10] Barrett sees Nietzsche himself as a kind of culture hero; he would attempt to take on the problem of living in a godless universe to give an example of the necessary courage: "He chose, that is, to suffer the conflict within his own culture in its most acute form and was eventually torn apart by it." After his emotional breakdown, during the long period of hospital convalescence, Nietzsche signed almost all his correspondence, "the crucified one."

Nietzsche's madman introduces a world that has lost, not only its gods and its myths, but its sense of order as well. The death of God was the death of Order, or so it seemed for a while, and Western literature in the twentieth century has, to a great extent, chronicled that death and recorded the effort to find some meaning in the wasteland that was left. T. S. Eliot's 1922 poem practically defines the intellectual and spiritual

---

[10]William Barrett, *Irrational Man: A Study in Existential Philosophy* (Garden City NY: Doubleday, 1962), p. 204.

landscape of the postwar years. With a vision of order, with the certainty
of order in earlier ages, Eliot says, life was fresh and meaningful, and man's
aspirations counted for something. But modern man seemed suddenly to
have been placed in a desert world with no sense of direction. Eliot's
images recall the passion of Christ, but in the parched world he describes,
neither water nor blood from the old religion can offer much relief:

> After the torchlight red on sweaty faces
> After the frosty silence in the gardens
> After the agony in stoney places
> The shouting and the crying
> Prison and palace and reverberation
> Of thunder of spring over distant mountains
> He who was living is now dead.
> We who were living are now dying.
> With a little patience.
> Here is no water but only rock
> Rock and no water and the sandy road
> The road winding above among the mountains
> Which are mountains of rock without water.

Water is an age-old symbol for life, rebirth, and renewal, and Eliot links
water (or the lack of it) with the slain god whose sacrifice can offer no
renewal in the modern world. In another section, "The Burial of the
Dead," one of the speakers in the poem asks a mocking question about the
sacrificed figure (who is as much a figure out of a pagan fertility rite as he
is a crucified Christ):

> . . . Stetson!
> You who were with me in the ships at Mylae!
> That corpse you planted last year in your garden,
> Has it begun to sprout? Will it bloom this year?
> Or has the sudden frost disturbed its bed?

In an age of vitality for the old myths—myths about a crucified
savior, a "hanged man," or the victim of some gruesome, primitive,
fertility rite—death could offer renewal or regeneration. The death of the
hero, of the man who suffers for all of us, *meant* something. Out of death
and out of suffering came hope and new life. But what came from the

deaths of all the heroes buried after the slaughter of the First World War? What pattern of renewal could we find? The question Eliot's speaker asks is mocking because it suggests its own terrible answer: now the slain figures do not rise and offer new life; they only rot.

Once Milton had attempted to assert eternal providence and justify the ways of God to man, but modern poets like Archibald MacLeish, dealing with the same problems of good and evil that Milton had pondered, but without Milton's vital mythic structure, seemed intent on asserting eternal accident and steeling man to the knowledge that the whole universe can offer man no "ways" that can be made to seem justifiable to anyone but a lunatic. One of the characters in MacLeish's play *J. B.* chants an ironic catechism:

> If God is God he is not good;
> If God is good he is not God.
> Take the even, take the odd.

And J. B.'s wife tells him at the end of the play what Matthew Arnold had said years before, that in the face of the loss of God, human beings can only turn to each other. "Blow on the coal of the heart," she tells her husband. "The candles in the churches are all out."

Interestingly enough, science contributed further to the general feelings of loss and of uncertainty by undermining, at this very time, even the belief in the reliability of the senses. The effect in the scientific community itself must have been a little like that of the effect of such startling sixteenth-century statements as "two bodies of unequal weight will fall through space at the same rate," or "the earth is not the center of the universe, and moves." Even common sense and everyday observation seem called into question here. After the work of Albert Einstein and Niels Bohr at the close of the first decade of this century, it was apparent to physicists and philosophers alike that anything approaching certainty must always be beyond human grasp. This was not due to the lack of precision of our instruments; it was due rather to the very nature of phenomena.

Discovery after discovery in physics and mathematics, especially, suggested that, while we may be able to ask more and more searching questions and receive ever more interesting answers, there is no way to achieve certainty. Perhaps the two best discussions of these discoveries for laymen are in Lincoln Barnett's book *The Universe and Dr. Einstein* and Jacob Bronowski's *The Ascent of Man*, but an interesting essay published in 1929 tells something of the impact of the new findings on the intellectual community of the time. The essay is entitled "The Downfall of Classical Physics," and it forms a chapter in a book by A. S. Eddington called *The Nature of the Physical World.*

The reports of scientists like Einstein and Rutherford and Bohr, says Eddington, give "an abrupt jar to those who think that things are more or less what they seem. The revelation by modern physics of the void within the atom is more disturbing than the revelation by astronomy of the immense void of interstellar space." Taking as an example the so-called "Fitzgerald Contraction," which asserts that the reliability of any device for measuring distance (or space) is entirely dependent on the direction and velocity of the motion of the observer—or, as he calls it, the observer's "frame of space"—Eddington quite convincingly demonstrates that our ability to answer the most basic questions about material objects is limited by our rather arbitrary method of picturing those objects in space. The limitation is not at all owing to the imperfection of our measuring tools, but to the very structure of matter.

"It would seem," Eddington says, "that all the forces of nature are entered into a conspiracy to prevent our discovering the location of any object; . . . naturally they cannot reveal it, if it does not exist." Our most basic beliefs in the perceivability of order are undermined by the discovery that "there is no guarantee that our methods of measuring lengths are not subject to a systematic kind of error. Worse still, we do not know if the error occurs or not, and there is every reason to presume that it is impossible to know."[11]

---

[11]A. S. Eddington, *The Nature of the Physical World* (Macmillan and Company, 1929).

I think it never occurred to anyone in the long line of scientists from Aristotle to Isaac Newton that it was "impossible to know"—not beyond our reach now, not difficult because of our present situation, but *impossible* to know. This is a thoroughly modern idea, and it echoes over and over again in the literature abut twentieth-century science. The physicist Werner Heisenberg, dealing with the argument (as old as the theories of Democritus and Plato) over whether the ultimate structure of things is based on tiny, indivisible units of matter or on something else, something more like the "forms" of Plato, says, "I think that our modern physics has definitely decided with Plato. In fact these smallest units of matter are not physical objects in the ordinary sense; they are forms, ideas, which can be expressed unambiguously only in mathematical language."[12] In his excellent little book on Einstein, Lincoln Barnett says, "What the scientist and the philosopher call the world of reality . . . is a skeleton structure of symbols, . . . and upon examination such concepts as gravitation, electro-magnetism, energy, current, momentum, the atom, the neutron, all turn out to be theoretical substructures, inventions, metaphors." Man attempting to find definite answers to his questions, says Barnett, "is somewhat in the position of a blind man trying to discern the shape and texture of a snowflake. As soon as it touches his fingers, it dissolves."[13]

All this is not to say that the findings of twentieth-century physics served to undermine a mythic structure in just the way the observations of Copernicus had. (The very language of a physicist like Heisenberg suggests the necessity of a mythico-symbolic approach to reality.) It is only to say that the feelings of uncertainty that Nietzsche had described were by no means a literary invention but an echo, a mirror, of the problem as it exists in the perception of twentieth-century man. Poets and novelists, after all, do not deal with abstractions but with the human reaction to problems and situations.

---

[12]*Natural Law and the Structure of Matter* (London: Rebel Press, 1970), p. 32.

[13]*The Universe and Dr. Einstein* (New York: Bantam Books, 1957), p. 115.

I mentioned in the first chapter a short story by Ernest Hemingway called "A Clean, Well-Lighted Place," and I should like to return briefly to it now. In the story, an old man drinks alone at a table in a cafe late at night while two waiters discuss him. The older one shares with the old man a desire for order, decency, and dignity—values he can impose on the void he sees when he is alone:

> What did he fear? It was not fear or dread. It was a nothing that he knew too well. It was all a nothing and a man was nothing too. It was only that and light was all it needed and a certain cleanness and order. Some lived in it and never felt it but he knew it all was nada y pues nada y nada y pues nada. Our nada, who are in nada, nada be thy name. . . . Hail nothing, full of nothing, nothing is with thee.

What does one do in the face of nothing? One desperately imposes order on it, by staying in the light, as the old man does, or by fighting a bull in a ring, as Pedro Romero does in *The Sun Also Rises*. (Bullfights and the like are not hairy-chested gestures in Hemingway's stories, but complex symbols of the imposition of order on a world that has no order of its own.) The poet W. H. Auden once complained that one element making the artistic vocation more difficult than it used to be is "the loss of belief in the significance and reality of sensory phenomena." We can no longer even believe our senses, much less the old myths that displayed for us the order that our senses apprehended. Thus the ancient idea of art as *mimesis* is destroyed, for there is no longer any nature "out there" to be imitated. In such a world, it is up to the artists and writers (who are, in all societies, the mythographers) to make order out of the chaos, to impose form on the void. In the process, if they are successful, some of them may find or invent myths that work.

Chapter 3

Reaching
For Myths

*The sun is but
a morning star.*
—HENRY DAVID THOREAU

W<small>HEN THE WANDERERS FROM</small> northern and central Europe first invaded the islands and mainland of the Aegean area about 1900 B.C., they brought with them their own chief deity, a decidedly male figure named Zeus. He was a weather god, a god of the sky, and the earliest depictions we have of him show him with his thunderbolt. The wanderers, some of whose descendants would be among the Greeks of the Classical Period many centuries later, settled among a people who worshiped an earth goddess, a dark, mysterious figure probably associated early with the mystery of fecundity or productivity in nature and later with childbirth. Homer tells us that her favorite cities were Argos, Sparta, and Mycenae, the last of which was, of course, the city of Agamemnon, the leader of the Greek forces in the Trojan War. By Homer's time this goddess, Hera, was the wife of Zeus, and a nearly constant antagonist with him, always quarreling over his love affairs, even siding against him in the major battles of Troy. The marriage of Zeus and Hera is an example of the *hieros gammos*, or sacred marriage, that unites two chief deities or (in the allegorizing tradition of the late medieval period, when Italian artists and writers, especially, were turning to the classical tradition for much of their inspiration) that unites two natural principles such as heaven and earth. What happened, according to most scholars, was that in the centuries between the coming of the Northern invaders and the writing of Homer the earth-goddess of the conquered people was married off to (and subordinated to) the sky-god of the conquerors. The frequent marital squabbles which Homer reports are the ghostly mythic record of the imperfect compromise between the invaders and the original inhabitants of the land that is now Greece.

Precisely this sort of marriage appears over and over again in numerous mythic traditions. We see it in such unions as that of Baal-Ishtar or Baal-Astarte in Mesopotamian and Phoenician lore. (A notable exception is the Judeo-Christian tradition which adamantly refused any sort of compromise represented by the *hieros gammos*. The closest thing to a female deity in either the Old or New Testament is the Virgin Mary, and her veneration dates from the medieval period—chiefly in France—long after Christianity had become established to the exclusion of all other traditions in the area. Anglo-Saxon translations of the gospels, fascinating as they are in their portrayal of Christ as a ring-giver and the disciples as his thanes, offer no attempt to unite the chief deities of the Northern world with Christianity.)

When one tradition supplants another, a marriage often ensues, suggesting an accomodation as aspects of one system are infused with another. Sometimes the marriage is literal (as in the union of Zeus and Hera) and often produces divine or semidivine offspring. (The union of Zeus and Demeter, another earth-grain-fertility figure, produces a daughter, Persephone, who later becomes goddess of the underworld.) Occasionally the accomodation is suggested by the simple merging of certain minor elements of ritual, as in Christians celebrating the human birth of their god during the time of the old Roman Saturnalia and even adopting some pagan accouterments in the celebration. As a tradition begins to lose its power over the imagination, the various deities assume lesser roles, often becoming subordinate to the deities of the tradition which supplants them, and occasionally becoming mere mortals. (The term "faded deities" refers to figures who were once regarded as gods or goddesses but whose importance lessened to such an extent that they became, in later myths, only humans. One might think of it as the opposite of Euhemerism, in which important human beings become elevated in myths to the status of gods.)

But what happens when a tradition simply runs out of steam, when it loses its vitality and power over the imagination without being supplanted immediately by any other system? Such a condition existed in Rome during the first and second centuries, A.D. Some Christians think of the struggles of the early church as a series of pitched battles against a firmly entrenched state religion, but this is an inaccurate picture. In fact, first-and-second-century Christianity was only one of dozens of relatively minor cults, and the church had as many bitter quarrels with its own heretical branches, such as the Gnostic, as it did with the worshipers of Jove or Bacchus. What caused the Christians to run afoul of Roman authority was their hard-headed and (it must have seemed to the Romans) rather uncharitable insistence, not just on the legitimacy of their own religion, but on the worthlessness of every other tradition— including the veneration of the emperor. Such narrow-minded fanaticism seemed startling and subversive to the usually lenient overseers of what Christians and Jews now refer to as The Holy Land. (The same exclusivist tendency is shared by the other major offshoot of Judaism, Islam.) Classical Greek and Roman religions were, for the most part, entirely tolerant of whatever quaint cult might grow up around them, and official Roman policy allowed any conquered nation to retain its own religion as long as it paid proper homage to Rome. Unfortunately for what William Butler Yeats once called "Platonic tolerance," however, it is usually the fanatics, not the logical, open-minded, and tolerant liberals, who make history, even if the road to history is through martyrdom. It is important to realize that the early Christians were seen as a threat to Roman civil authority rather than as a threat to Roman religion.

By the end of the first century, A.D.—by the time of Ovid, in other words—no single cult could be said to dominate Roman religious traditions. Ovid was a wonderful gatherer of tales from dozens of older sources, ranging from Homer and Hesiod through the fifth-century playwrights to the Alexandrine poets and many others. He was a master storyteller, witty and amusing, always fresh. He quite plainly believed none of what he told—that is, believed in the sense that Paul believed in the historicity of the resurrection— and his tales were decorative and delightful and purported to be nothing else. Furthermore, the audience for which he wrote was as urbane and sophisticated as any audience in Western civilization has ever been, and it shared his view of the stories about gods and goddesses as mere decorative inventions. Some traditions, true enough, were alive. Most people still believed that the future could be told by consulting an oracle such as the famous one at Delphi, and the temples of major deities such as Mars or Jove were still important places of worship; but the power of almost all individual myths had waned to such an extent that Rome had, in a sense, no single, coherent mythic vision. Certainly it did not have the mythic coherency that had existed in Greece five hundred years earlier or that would exist again in Rome and in Byzantium five hundred years later.

Romans in general—at least the sophisticated Romans whom Ovid addressed—were no more likely to believe in the literal truth of Ovid's charming story of Cupid and Psyche than most sophisticated people of the twentieth century are to believe in the equally charming story of the creation of Eve. A good story was one thing, but getting overwrought about the historicity of the story was quite another. Doubtless Paul's letter to the Laodiceans, in which he rails at them for being lukewarm, was a reaction to just this kind of take-it-or-leave-it attitude. (We do not have any letters of the Laodiceans addressed to Paul, but if we did we would probably find that they regarded the man as a wild-eyed fanatic.) Certainly the defensiveness of the very early Christian writers who insist that their story is true and all others are just stories is a calculated effort to deal with the inevitable comparisons to be made between the resurrection of Christ, for instance, and the rebirth of Dionysus. (Paul himself said that if things didn't happen just exactly the way they were supposed to have happened, the whole effort of the church was a colossal waste of time. Some bitter struggles in the early church centered on whose version of what happened was the true version.) Clearly, Christianity was an idea whose time had come—if only because so many other ideas had already come and gone and their going had left a kind of mythic vacuum.

By the beginning of the third century, after Constantine had made his sudden decision to declare Christianity the official religion of the empire, the fortunes of the new religion were made. What had begun as a small group of extremists and visionaries in a corner of the empire had, in less than 300 years, so completely triumphed over the old system (or systems) that the most venerated traditions of Greece and Rome became merely stories. This was because Rome had lost the thread of its own mythic tradition, a tradition that had made sense of the world for over 1,000 years. Not a single major piece of it remained as a vital part of the tradition that replaced it.

This is exactly the situation Yeats describes so vividly in "The Second Coming" and "Two Songs From a Play." His description is tailored to fit not only first-century Rome, but the twentieth-century Western world as well. In the first poem, the aimlessness of a civilization whose myths are wearing out is symbolized by the rising spiral ("gyre") of a falcon which has gone beyond the control of the falconer. The poem ends with a question about the nightmarish vision of whatever new order must come: "And what rough beast, its hour come round at last, / Slouches towards Bethlehem to be born?" The first of the "Two Songs From a Play" offers a vision of the rebirth of the slain god Dionysus (symbolic of the old religion) in the new cult of Christ:

I saw a staring virgin stand
Where holy Dionysus died,
And tear the heart out of his side,
And lay the heart upon her hand
And bear that beating heart away;
And then did all the muses sing
Of Magnus Annus in the spring
As though God's death were but a play.

Yeats's vision of the wearing-out of traditional myth in the twentieth century encompasses not only the decay of religion, but the loss of a
whole body of secular beliefs as well. Ever since the Renaissance, the faith
(in the largest sense) of Western man has been a complex combination of
natural and supernatural tendencies of thought. One example of this
combination is the tendency of many people in the nineteenth century to
apply the Darwinian theories of evolution to social and cultural phenomena or even to morality. (Most Social Darwinists conveniently over-
looked the fact that evolution does not mean change for the better; it
simply means change.) Tennyson's enthusiastic and rather theatrical
young speaker in "Locksley Hall," for instance, works himself to a fever
pitch over the possibilities of change, especially change brought about
through the scientific advances of the modern world:

> Not in vain the distance beacons. Forward, forward
>   let us range,
> Let the great world spin forever down the ringing grooves
>   of change.
> Through the shadow of the globe we sweep into the
>   younger day:
> Better fifty years of Europe than a cycle of Cathay.

What the speaker implies here is the belief (common in Tennyson's
day as well as in our own) that Western man, benefited as he is by the
Enlightenment, by his sciences, by his sophisticated technology (such as
the train which provides the powerful but somewhat confusing metaphor, "the ringing grooves of change") is immeasurably better—not just
more comfortable, not just better off, but better—than the benighted
millions of the world who never heard of Sir Isaac Newton. To doubt that
this kind of belief was anything less than an article of faith for multitudes
of nineteenth-century believers is to underestimate the power of the
human species for myopia. A humorous example of it appears much later
in the *Tarzan* series of Edgar Rice Burroughs. Tarzan, who cannot
remember ever having seen a European and who is provided on every
hand with examples of savagery and cruelty, refuses to eat the flesh of a
fallen human adversary because he knows *instinctively* that cannibalism is

wrong. He knows this because he is white, because he is English—and not just ordinary English, mind you, but a member of the nobility. Tarzan, after all, is really Lord Greystoke, and blood will tell.

We may smile at Burroughs's naiveté, but the implications of it are far from funny. Such an attitude makes possible the development of a formidable mythic system regarding the white man's burden. It also makes possible and even necessary the kind of brutal colonial exploitation that Joseph Conrad details vividly in *Heart of Darkness*. The comfortable illusion that God's plan included an eventual restructuring of the whole world (one might say the gradual evolution) along the lines of the model He had created in the industrialized countries of the West was a firmly entrenched point of belief during the Colonial period, and it remains as an article of faith for many today.

The fusion of a popular scientific idea such as evolution with religion and social concerns is only one example of the complex mixture of beliefs that have gone to make up the order perceived by Western man and embodied in his myths. In fact, if it had only been the religious mythological system that was eroded so seriously by the end of the second decade of the twentieth century, modern society might more easily have weathered the storm by placing an increased trust in its most cherished secular myths. Unfortunately, it was not merely a specific religious view of order or even religion in general that seemed to be falling apart in the early years of this century; order itself was in danger. As I have suggested in chapter two, even the findings of scientists and mathematicians pointed to a disquieting revaluation of the way in which we might look at the most common natural phenomena. The old standards no longer seemed adequate for assessing the modern experience. This was the case in religion, in politics, in psychology, and in science; the clearest expression of it is to be found in modern art and literature.

When writers like T. S. Eliot and I. A. Richards complained of the vagueness and the lofty sentimentality of certain of their nineteenth-century predecessors (especially Tennyson, Wordsworth, and Shelley), they were reacting to a world that had changed so drastically that the

approaches to it must also change. The vision of human perfectibility that
Shelley nourished from time to time seemed childishly and even perverse-
ly wrongheaded to the generation of writers springing up after 1918. A
fine example of this kind of impatience occurs in William Faulkner's
Light in August. Faulkner has Gail Hightower, a sentimental escapist from
the modern world, sitting in his den reading a volume of Tennyson's
poetry. After reaching emotional maturity, however, and learning to
accept the hard facts and responsibilities of human existence, Hightower
throws away his Tennyson and pulls out a copy of Shakespeare's *Henry
IV.* The moderns had no time for what they considered the maundering
sensibilities of an age that had failed to see (or worse, had chosen to
ignore) the facts of human loneliness, isolation, and insecurity. In *A
Farewell to Arms* Hemingway rails against the use of words like sacred,
glorious, and sacrifice because in the face of the loss of order the words
made no sense:

> I had seen nothing sacred, and the things that were glorious had no glory
> and the sacrifices were like the stockyards at Chicago if nothing was done
> with the meat except to bury it. There were many words that you could
> not stand to hear and finally only the names had dignity. Certain numbers
> were the same way and certain dates and these with the names of places
> were all you could say and have them mean anything. Abstract words
> such as glory, honor, courage, or hallow were obscene beside the concrete
> names of villages, the numbers of roads, the names of rivers, the numbers
> of regiments, and the dates.

Hemingway here, as elsewhere, shows a fascination with the
concreteness of objects, with the most elemental and palpable aspects of
experience, that typifies much of the literature of the period. Experiments
with imagism and haiku in poetry point to the same kind of fascination.
The writers seemed to have lost or abandoned the notion of writing about
ideas and to have turned, as Husserl would put it, "to the things
themselves," as if in an effort to start their thinking afresh. But the
question remained to them, "What can we believe?" Myths must grow
out of patterns of belief, and all men, even the most modern men, must
believe in something.

If we focus on the major belief systems of American society during the twentieth century, we find a fascinating array of both secular and religious elements, many of which have been in a state of flux for much of the century. Some of these mythic elements (or variations of them) are common to Western society in general, but quite a few of them are distinctly American. The United States is among the most thoroughly industrialized and scientific nations in the world, and anyone with an inadequate understanding of how mythology works might question the idea that we are much concerned with myths. In fact, Americans tend to cherish and believe in their myths, both the religious or quasi-religious and the purely secular, as zealously as any society has ever protected its own system of ordering the world. Even the country's founding is both a part of national mythic imagination and a major source of its myth-making energy.

In the first place, the United States is a product of the Enlightenment in a sense that no other country is. Its progenitors and first heroes were rational men who believed that the human intellect was sufficient to solve all problems. Except for the men of the battlefield or the frontier (and to an extent, even there) the heroes of mythic or near-mythic proportions are heroes of practicality, of the intellect, and of the rational spirit of man—men like Franklin, Jefferson, and Paine. (Paine could be as irrationally stubborn and dogmatic as any of the people he ridiculed, but at least in the popular estimation he has become a practical and supremely rational man.) Americans have traditionally attached a tremendous importance to the capabilities of the rational mind for working out any problems whatsoever. In elevating the intellect—and especially the practical, American intellect—to this lofty place Americans have often tended to ignore the sheer perversity of human character and the fact that some problems do not lend themselves to rational solutions. There is a wonderful anecdote about a conversation between Jean Paul Sartre and an American intellectual. The two disagreed; finally Sartre gave up the effort to talk with the man, as their positions were wholly irreconcilable.

"The problem is," said Sartre, "I believe in the existence of evil, and he does not."[1]

In the second place, the United States has always been conscious of its own beginnings as a nation in a way that few other countries are and that no European country is. There is a mythic element about the founding of the country that was already being recognized and celebrated decades—even a century—before the Articles of Peace were signed in 1783. England and France, by way of contrast, grew for centuries toward becoming England and France. Those countries have a long, rich, and colorful history and a longer "prehistory," as it were, while America tends to regard itself as having sprung almost magically from the sweat and blood and imagination of a handful of freedom-loving, intelligent visionaries. The result of this unique inception is a reinforcement of the idea that intelligent, reasonable, resourceful people can accomplish absolutely anything—human perversity and luck be damned. This is an oversimplification, of course, but it is not a very gross one.

Furthermore, certain peculiar, quasi-religious aspects of the country's founding have profoundly influenced the national mythic consciousness. William Bradford and some of the other early Puritan leaders insisted on calling the place "New Jerusalem," and, while nobody except the Puritans took very seriously the idea of America as a theocracy, the concept of a New Eden, the place for a whole new beginning that would regenerate the world, has proved a potent one.[2] We must view this attitude in relation to the faith in human reason and the myths of the creation of the entire nation out of chaos, so to speak, in some one

---

[1]Quoted in William Barrett, p. 273. In the same chapter, "The Place of the Furies," Barrett comments at length on the American tendency to ignore or deny the existence of evil and the insolubility of certain problems, and of the possibility of tragic consequences in that ignorance or denial. Interestingly, he also points to an identical failing in Marxist philosophy—which, like American idealism, fails utterly to take into account any but objective and social obstacles to man's ultimate perfection.

[2]For a discussion of the tremendous impact of this idea on American literature, see especially R. W. B. Lewis, *The American Adam: Innocence, Tragedy, and Tradition in the Nineteenth Century* (Chicago: University of Chicago Press, 1955).

hundred fifty years. ("Let there be freedom," said the Continental Congress, and there was freedom.) Seen this way, the mere facts of the country's founding add up to a fertile ground for myth-making.

Finally, the physical geography of the United States lends itself to a certain kind of myth-making and myth-reinforcing. Its tremendous size and variety, with climates ranging from subarctic to semitropical, and its physical isolation from its European origins have always influenced the country's awareness of itself. It is not, as England is, exactly an island nation, but its separation from Europe by over two thousand miles of ocean engenders that impression. Most Americans remain fairly ignorant of the history or traditions of Canada or Mexico (they probably know more about those of France, Italy, or Germany) although they would tend to regard both countries as sharing the unique destiny of being part of the "new" world. Perhaps one reason why American presidents have regarded the possible incursion of communism into any nation on this side of the Atlantic as a real and immediate threat to the security of the United States is that they have been accustomed to think of the entire western hemisphere as at least a geographic if not a political and ideological extension of the United States. The threat may be real enough, for a number of economic and military reasons, but the geographical egocentrism involved might either amuse or outrage other countries, depending on their own ideological disposition. In recent months, El Salvador has been in the news because of the conflict between a repressive central government and a communist-backed opposition party which has been waging a guerilla war. With some reluctance, the United States government has been supporting the government in El Salvador because of fears regarding the consequences of a communist takeover in any other nation in this hemisphere. San Salvador, the capital, is almost as far from Washington as London is from Moscow—a geographical fact that must puzzle many European observers of United States foreign policy.

There is in America no single, coherent mythic system, but rather a complex interplay of traditions, many of them contradictory. In that sense, at least, our condition resembles that of first-century Rome.

Leaving aside the American Judeo-Christian mythic tradition (which is not in any important way different from the religious traditions of other nations), we might lump most of the major secular belief systems of this country into a single category called The Myth of the New Beginning. This includes primarily the belief that the essence of the American experience is the fresh start, the chance to escape from the mistakes and shortcomings of past societies, to create not exactly a New Jerusalem (as Bradford would have wanted), but certainly a secular and humane version of that ideal. The virtues of the New Beginning are change, youth, experimentation, and boundless optimism. They are values which are reflected again and again in our art and literature, which are a part of our way of looking at politics, history, and both the social and the natural sciences, and which are little less than articles of faith for the vast majority of Americans.

The poet and high priest of the New Beginning was Walt Whitman, who called himself a new Adam and urged Americans to celebrate with him the limitless potential of the new American self. He promised "to define America, her athletic Democracy," and said that all his songs were of the "Modern Man." The expression of precisely this kind of heady literary enthusiasm about the American experience goes back much further than Whitman, however; at least as early as the 1790s writers like Charles Brockden Brown were urging a national literature that would capitalize on the uniqueness of what was sometimes called the American "experiment." Brown went so far as to say in a letter to a European friend that no one from the Old World could possibly understand an American book since the essential experience in this country simply defied translation.

In fact, Europeans themselves often cherished a similar idea about America, from the time of the early colonists up to the beginning of the nineteenth century. The Jean Jacques Rousseau school of noble savagery influenced Europeans to regard the New World as a place of primal innocence, an Edenic wilderness to be enjoyed by any sensitive Adam or

Eve who might wish to make the journey.[3] (This sort of sentimentalizing of primitive societies is by no means out of date. When anthropologists in the Philippines reported a decade or so ago that they had found a small tribe of people who had had no contact with anyone outside their isolated valley, the point journalists found most fascinating was that the tribe had no word for "war." That a tribe of thirty or so people living in complete isolation on a tropical island has no word for war should be no more surprising than that it also has no word for refrigerator, but modern Rousseaus took the finding as a sure indication of the moral superiority of primitive men and women.) One recalls the ill-fated Pantisocracy that a small group of English writers and intellectuals had planned on the banks of the Susquehanna River. The idealism broke down when Coleridge and Southey quarreled over how many servants Southey could take to a perfect democracy, and all Coleridge got out of the bargain was a wife with whom he could never get along, but the mere existence of the plan indicates the seriousness with which Englishmen took the idea of the New Beginning. Particularly during the Romantic Era, major writers in England helped to form—or at least to reinforce—the new nation's concept of itself. Blake's powerful poem "America: A Prophecy" was not widely distributed either here or in England during his lifetime, but similar sentiments in the works of other Romantic writers did not escape notice in America in the early 1800s.

Two other eloquent supporters of the New Beginning in the first half of the nineteenth century were Ralph Waldo Emerson and Henry David Thoreau. While both men, as Romantic Transcendentalists, would naturally have considered themselves more or less in opposition to the strict rationalism of men like Franklin (Thoreau's *Walden* even mocks, at times, the very language of Franklin's *Autobiography*), the emphasis on individual genius, on Yankee ingenuity—finally, on what Emerson called simply "self-reliance," puts them squarely in the mainstream of American

---

[3]Rousseau's savages were only one aspect of the white man's series of stereotypes about the American Indian. See Oliver LaFarge, "Myths that Hide the American Indian," *American Heritage* 7 (October 1956).

optimism.[4] They urge an acceptance of whatever task might come to hand, confident that the resourceful individual, the new Adam, can effect changes leading to a better world. A single paragraph from "Self-Reliance" indicates the recurrent theme in the work of both men:

> Trust thyself: every heart vibrates to that iron string. Accept the place the divine providence has found for you, the society of your contemporaries, the connection of events. Great men have always done so, and confided themselves childlike to the spirit of their age, betraying their perception the absolutely trustworthy was seated at their heart, working through their hands, predominating in all their being. And we are now men, and must accept in the highest mind the same transcendent destiny; and not minors and invalids in a protected corner, not cowards fleeing before a revolution, but guides, redeemers and benefactors, obeying the Almighty effort and advancing on Chaos and the Dark.

Now this is heady stuff—the clear trumpet-call of individual effort, the affirmation of the power of the individual intellect to triumph over all adversity and overcome all problems. It occurs over and over again in Emerson and in Thoreau, who ends his best-known work with an elaborate metaphor about a "beautiful and winged life, whose egg has been buried for ages under many concentric layers of woodenness in the dead dry life of society," finally bursting forth "to enjoy its perfect summer life at last." It is out of this background, with its emphasis on growth and its spirit of optimism, that the poet-priest Whitman steps, filled with precisely this spirit and chanting it enthusiastically, like a worshiper in a dream vision of the New Beginning:

> This day before dawn I ascended a hill and look'd at
>   the crowded heaven,
> And I said to my spirit When we have become the enfolders
>   of these orbs, and the pleasure and knowledge of

---

[4]This is, I realize, an oversimplification of Emerson's thought. For a full understanding of Emerson, one must balance essays like "Self-Reliance" and "Nature" with others like "Fate" and "Experience." Still, his most important work, in his own day and in ours, is surely in the early essays. Most of his contemporaries certainly thought so; Herman Melville satirized his optimism in *The Confidence Man* (1857).

everything in them, shall we be filled and satisfied then?
And my spirit said No, but we but level that lift to
    pass and continue beyond.
            . . . . .
Sit a while dear son,
Here are biscuits to eat and here is milk to drink,
But as soon as you sleep and renew yourself in sweet
    clothes, I kiss you with a good-bye kiss and open
    the gates for your egress hence.
Long enough have you dreamed contemptible dreams,
Now I wash the gum from your eyes,
You must habit yourself to the dazzle of light and of
    every moment of your life.
Long have you timidly waded holding a plank by the shore,
Now I will you to be a bold swimmer,
To jump off in the midst of the sea, rise again, nod
    to me, shout, and laughingly dash with your hair.

What we see here, in the work of Emerson, Thoreau, and Whitman, is the unequivocal expression of that optimism about American possibilities, that confidence in modernity and the American "experiment," that was an essential element in the pattern of mythic beliefs since the founding of the nation. The "Frontier Thesis" of the historian Frederick Jackson Turner is merely a study of another aspect of this belief in growth and optimism about the recurrent possibilities of the New Beginning. I believe it is significant that the novels of Herman Melville (who, with Hawthorne, was inclined toward a more tragic vision of human potential than were Emerson and the transcendentalists) never found a real audience until after the First World War. The society that could embrace Eliot and Hemingway was at last ready for Melville. The optimistic belief in the New Beginning was by this time not the only dominant mythic strain in our society, but it was still powerful and it remains so today.

Chapter 4

Beginning and Returning

The end is where
we start from.
—T. S. ELIOT

N̲O MYTHIC THEME IS more appealing than the theme of renewal, and that is why we find in almost every mythology the suggestion of the possibility of a new beginning. For the Hindus, the theme of destruction and regeneration is so central and all-pervasive that an outsider must understand something about Hindu cosmology before he can appreciate the most basic traditions surrounding even one of the major deities. God is the creator of not just one but a succession of universes; in one of his aspects he is Vishnu, asleep on the back of a serpent in the cosmic ocean between creations. Waking again and again, he shapes worlds which last for billions of years and then cease to exist as the god takes his rest once more. World after world is born and dies as he assumes a succession of avatars. There is no beginning and there is no end, only a cycle of deaths and rebirths, destruction and renewal. More than any other mythic traditions, the great religions of India emphasize the union of the creative and destructive forces in the universe.

The Hindus refer to the absolute reality, the all-encompassing existence of which everything else—including individual human lives—

is a part, as *Brahman*. All things come from *Brahman*, including what we could call the physical universe, and all things return to *Brahman*. The physical world, called *maya*, is merely a projection of *Brahman*, a temporary manifestation which lasts a little over four trillion years and then ceases to exist, being reborn again in another cycle: worlds without end, forever. The chief three dieties in Hindu mythology suggest aspects of the process—Brahma is the creator of worlds; Vishnu the sustainer; Shiva the destroyer. Indian mythology is home to a bewildering array of minor dieties and demigods, but these are the chief three. To Western minds, Shiva is perhaps the most confusing. He is often represented in art as riding a bull or as dancing. His dance is the ceaseless movement of all things in the universe, the movement to destruction and thence to recreation and reincarnation. Various attributes of Shiva (especially the bull on which he rides and the lingam, or phallus, often associated with his worship) suggest his generative, life-giving powers. His wife is called Shakti; she is also known by other names—Parvoti, Durga, Kali. As Kali, or Kali Ma, the dark mother, she is the terrifying goddess of destruction, associated with epidemics, floods, earthquakes, and storms. In paintings and statues, Kali is a dark woman with four arms. In one hand she holds a sword, in another a severed head; the other two hands beckon to her worshipers. Her earrings are two corpses and she wears a necklace of human skulls hanging below her blood-stained breasts. Shakti (or Durga-Uma-Parvoti-Kali), the divine mother, is the object of veneration at the largest and most elaborate of the Bengali festivals, the Durga Puja. In other words, it is not the rather distant creator figure, Brahma, and not the merry sustainer, Vishnu, but an aspect of the destroyer, Shiva, who figures most prominently in the autumnal celebrations of the Bengalis. This makes little sense to a mind conditioned by Western myths to see the world in terms of a struggle between the powers of light and creativity on the one hand and the powers of darkness and destruction on the other. Nevertheless, it makes perfectly good sense to a mind conditioned by Hindu thought to see all existence, all *maya*, as a dancing moment in the endless lives and deaths of god.

While the Indians fashioned around this mythic theme of destruction and renewal, the oldest extant religion in the world, the majority of
other traditions have at least paid nodding service to the same concept.
Even the mythology of northern Europe, which predicted the eventual
destruction of gods and men together at *ragnarok*, also pointed to a new
creation that would succeed the combined fire and flood of destruction.
For Christians, the idea of personal renewal is paramount; the Apostles'
Creed, a statement of the faith of the worshiper in most Christian
churches, concludes with an affirmation of just that renewal: "I believe in
. . . the resurrection of the body, and the life everlasting." The language of
Christianity is filled with references to renewal and rebirth; the ceremony
of baptism is as much a death-rebirth motif as it is a ritual enactment of
the cleansing power of Christ's sacrifice.

The theme of renewal is, in a very real sense, the most sacred tenet
of American mythology. This is not at all because the United States is a
predominantly Christian country; it is instead because of the unique
background of the nation. (See the discussion in chapter three.) The
essence of the American experience is the new start; the American is, as
Walt Whitman never got tired of pointing out, Adam beginning all over
again with a new garden—except that now he has invented the tractor.
One does not have to turn to major national literary figures to find the
theme presented, for like all truly mythic elements, it is a part of the folk
tradition. It is so deeply ingrained in the way we see ourselves that we not
only fail to question it, we fail even to recognize it as a belief. Rather it is a
given, an indisputable constant, like the shape of a triangle or a square, or
the color of grass. America is the land of opportunity—which is only
another way of saying it is the land of renewal. We laugh at Horatio
Alger's art as a storyteller—the predictable outcomes, the moralizing, the
superficiality of characterization—but we believe in the mythic truth
behind the stories, even when the truth seems too simplistically handled.
The youth movement of the 1960s was sometimes depicted by its
detractors as being anti-American; the participants themselves were fond
of believing that they were struggling against the complacent beliefs of an

entrenched and self-satisfied America. In fact, however, the movement represented the very essence of American mythology, the wonderfully naive belief that there is a solution to every problem. We can just start over, Bob Dylan told us—and over and over and over. Shiva dances to the beat of the tambourine man.

A complementary facet of the theme of the New Beginning is the theme of the return. Both are, in fact, aspects of the same desire—the desire to correct present ills by reforming society or even humanity. Both are also an integral part of the American mythic vision and have been since the country's inception. As I mentioned in the previous chapter, the Puritan concept of a New Eden, a place where man could reestablish a primal relationship with God, has proved a potent one in our literature— and not just Puritan literature. American writers from Joel Barlowe to William Faulkner have dealt with the theme over and over again, and even when they point out where and how the dream failed (they almost always do), they recognize its effect on the national consciousness.[1] So potent is the myth that Americans now pay ritual obeisance to almost any manifestation of renewal or return. A wealthy family builds a log cabin (from precut, ready-to-assemble units) on the edge of a lake and grows a vegetable garden in the summer. An engineer leaves a promising career to raise corn and tobacco on a one-hundred-acre farm, taking along a third-year art student who weaves rugs and cans vegetables when she is

---

[1] In several stories in the *Go Down Moses* collection, especially "The Old People" and "The Bear," Faulkner writes about the failure of the dream because of man's greed (original sin?), which in the American South took the most insidious form, slavery. The Indian leader who dealt first with the whites in Mississippi was called by the French *L'homme* (the man); he is remembered by later generations as Doom (an anglicization of *de l'homme*—of the man).

Joel Barlowe's *Columbiad* (1807) is an ambitious epic dealing with the possibilities for regeneration and renewal in the New World. Barlowe had even Columbus full of enthusiasm about the Edenic possibilities, but human perversity and avarice spoil everything; a quarrel breaks out between the Europeans and the Indians, and there is bloodshed. The serpent is already in the garden, it seems, and man must invariably fall.

Hawthorne's opening scene in *The Scarlet Letter* shows the Puritan crowd flanked by a prison and a graveyard: *Et in Arcadia Ego.*

not working beside him in the fields. A professor of English wears jeans and work shirts and drives a pickup truck to work, having convinced himself that such clothing and transportation are the most practical and sensible available to him. Without being aware of participating in ritual acts, each of these people demonstrates his faith in and adherence to aspects of a myth that has always controlled, to a great extent, the way Americans see themselves.

Fully one half of the books on our best-seller lists are volumes purporting to give instructions in starting over, getting down to basics, and renewing the soul.[2] Bumper stickers and T-shirt slogans announce that today is the first day of the rest of our lives. Such an observation would seem, to the objective mind, a childishly obvious truth, but we nod agreement, feeling a chord struck somewhere deep within the self, deeper than logic or objectivity, in the region of the mind where myth works.

All this is not to say that Americans are more concerned, in their mythology, with the theme of renewal than other people are or have been, but we do seem to be more interested than others in the theme as it applies to each individual and to specific historical situations. Christianity looks toward the eventual purification of the world through the sacrifice of Christ, and individual Christians are "reborn" spiritually—but only once and only in one specific direction. The worldwide renewal in Hindu mythology is so unthinkably remote that the proper business of a Hindu devotee is to learn to accomodate himself to his present earthly circumstances. Traditions which stress acceptance of the will of the Almighty (Islam is a good example) provide for rapid change only in accordance with varying interpretations of that will. But for Americans, renewal is a way of life—one might almost say a sign of grace. Even as we fear change

---

[2]Another powerful influence on the American myth of renewal has been the Romantic emphasis on growth and change. All six major American authors (Emerson, Poe, Thoreau, Hawthorne, Melville, and Whitman) who were publishing before the Civil War were in the Romantic tradition, and each man tended to recognize and champion the importance of change. When we go to the farm or to the woods, we take Thoreau with us, whether or not we have bought his book.

(it is human nature both to fear the new and to loathe the everyday), we are fascinated by it and tend to believe that the future is always brighter—or can be made that way if we make the right decisions about renewal and return.

I believe our European counterparts are not as obsessed with and optimistic about the possibilities of renewal as we are. They tend not to believe, as we surely do believe, that there is an answer to every problem, if we can only be rational and unafraid to try new approaches to problem solving. Americans are disappointed if today is not as wonderful as yesterday or if tomorrow does not promise something even more grand. We expect things to improve because that is the natural order of things, and if there is no improvement there must be renewal. Some writers have suggested that this is because we were never exposed in quite the way all of Europe was exposed to the full horror of either the First or the Second World War. Americans suffered and died in both wars, to be sure, but England lost one-third of its male population between 1914 and 1918, and whole towns in France were completely depopulated. More Germans died in one night in 1945, when the city of Dresden was firebombed, than America lost in the entire Vietnam War.[3] Total German losses in the Second World War were over eight million dead or disabled, or about a tenth of the entire population, and losses in some of its neighboring countries were proportionately somewhat higher. Widespread confusion, the dislocation of large segments of the population, hunger, and disease took a toll that can only partially be reckoned by mere numbers on a page.

American losses were great (320,000 dead or disabled in the First World War, 460,000 in the Second), but they did not compare with those of the Europeans. We fought in both wars, and we buried our dead

---

[3]In fact, more people died in Dresden than in Nagasaki. The fire storm which swept the city as a result of the bombing killed between 75,000 and 150,000 people, many of them refugees from the Eastern Theatre of war. (By comparison, 140,000 were killed in the atomic bombing of Hiroshima, and 74,000 at Nagasaki; 58,000 Americans lost their lives in Vietnam.) Joseph Goebbels, the Nazi Minister of Propaganda, cited the fire bombing of Dresden as an inhuman atrocity, saying that such an unnecessary and wanton act proved beyond doubt the savagery and barbarity of the Americans.

and grieved, but as a nation we were spared the holocaust, the mind-wrenching vision of the full possibilities of destruction that was Europe's destiny. Such losses do not destroy optimism—even in one generation—and that is an indication of the amazing human potential for hope. But they temper it.

For the last decade or so, however, it has been interesting to recognize the steady undermining of faith in solutions. World War II was an immensely popular war; few people doubted the rightness of our involvement in it. (Those who protested—like the poet Robert Lowell—suffered the consequences.) The eventual Allied victory seemed little less than a nod from the Almighty himself indicating that we had done the right thing. We were rewarded with pictures of the concentration centers and death camps like Auschwitz, Belsen, and Dachau, feeding our sense of morality: surely this was proof that we had won a righteous war. (That we knew nothing of the death camps until the end of the war was a trivial fact that did not get in the way of the general principle. History is usually more interesting and always more clear-cut when it is written in reverse.)

But what was right and what was wrong in Vietnam? Had we simply left the country to its fate after the French withdrew, its corrupt little dictatorship would probably have fallen, the conquerors would have initiated bloody purges and set up a new kind of dictatorship, and several million people would have suffered terribly. Had we annihilated the opposition with all the force—perhaps even thermonuclear force—at our disposal, we would surely have killed, maimed, and left homeless, diseased, and starving millions of people, destroyed a tremendous amount of Eastern culture and heritage in Vietnam and in neighboring countries like Laos and Cambodia as well, to succeed only in propping up an ineffectual and popularly despised, repressive regime. We chose to strike a middle course, leading us to sacrifice fifty-eight thousand American lives, kill several times that many Vietnamese, lay waste much of the countryside, disrupt the economy, and then withdraw—whereupon the takeover that we had sought to prevent took place in a very short time, complete with purges and repression.

Our fighting men went into this war as Americans had gone into others—at least at first. But soon they found themselves portrayed, not only in the foreign press but in their own, as villains and aggressors, not patriots or defenders of freedom. The result was uniquely frustrating to American nineteen-year-olds home on leave who found themselves ostracized or (worse) pitied by their former friends, people who now marched in anti-war demonstrations and carried pictures of Ho Chi Minh. (The soldiers' fathers' friends had not carried pictures of Hirohito or Hitler. What was wrong?) Americans were unsure of the reasons for the war, which is only another way of saying that they were unsure of what was right. Then came the pictures of My Lai, and the public turned its back on Vietnam in sickness and disgust. So we left, and when we looked over our collective shoulder, we saw that Vietnam was no better off than it would have been if we had left earlier and perhaps not much worse than it would have been had we stayed. We lost more than a war then; we lost a conviction that we could know what was right. Then within a few months of the war's end, we found ourselves in the curious moral position of lending our support to Chinese efforts to reinstate the government of Pol Pot in Cambodia. Pol Pot's government was anti-Russian and anti-Vietnamese; it was also the most brutally repressive in recent memory. In an orgiastic purging of intellectuals and other undesirable elements of the civilian population, it tortured to death, buried alive in mass graves, and summarily executed between one million and three million people. In short, we found ourselves at least tacitly supporting organized horror and butchery on a scale that threatened to outdo anything the Third Reich had produced. "Where do we begin again from here?" we asked ourselves. "Where now do we turn for renewal?"

It is one thing to say that Americans are and always have been vitally interested in the idea of renewal. It is quite another to say that this idea constitutes a mythic theme. To what extent, or by what definition, one might ask, is there a myth of the New Beginning? If we define myths as tales which are believed to be true or at least are taken very seriously by a significant portion of a society and which are demonstrations of the order that a society perceives, then we can point to a whole collection of American tales which can justifiably be labeled myths of the New Beginning. We have only to look at the persistent popularity of any aspect of the "frontier" to understand the significance of the New Beginning in American thinking.[4]

Our folk heroes are rebels; they turn away from all that is traditional, comfortable, and everyday. The defenders of New Orleans in 1814 were riflemen from Kentucky and Tennessee, we are told. According to the most popular accounts, they were not highly skilled soldiers, but they were capable of nearly superhuman accuracy with their long-barreled rifles, being accomplished hunters and Indian fighters whose prowess and hardiness had been forged on the frontier. The Crocketts, Bridgers, and Boones of our nation's formative years are real enough, but they are also, in a sense, more than real, as mythic heroes always are. What they say to us is this: there is always renewal, always the chance for a new beginning. For the frontier hero, as for any hero, the journey involves the call to adventure (which hero was it—or was it each of them—who moved westward whenever he could see the smoke rising from a neighbor's chinmey?), the trials and suffering (hunger, the deaths of companions, battles with animal and human adversaries), and eventual apotheosis.

Nor is our celebration of the frontier ethic limited to the heroes of the eighteenth and nineteenth centuries; it permeates our politics, our diversions, and even some of the advertising by our large corporations. We pay homage to precisely this kind of thing when we nod in solemn agreement to The Getty Corporation's advertisements which portray the daring and typically American spirit of the modern business executive. We are shown an individual who must leave comfort and security behind

---

[4]While most historians now believe that Frederick Jackson Turner's "Frontier Thesis" of American history was an oversimplification, they grant the validity of the basic assumption: the presence—real or imagined—of a frontier, with its ever-appealing promise of a new beginning, was a powerful force in the shaping of the nation.

in search of greatness. If the Getty ads seem so farfetched that they make us smile (Jim Bridger in a three-piece suit?), it is only because our minds refuse to accept the link between the monolithic corporation and the lone individual. The important thing, though, is that both corporation and individual represent—according to Getty's ad writers—the American willingness to dare to begin anew, to explore the unknown for all our sakes.

Before much more can be said about particular types of American heroes, we must examine some of the implications for our society of the Myth of the New Beginning. There are five which are especially noteworthy.

In the first place, we have a predictable tendency to idealize youthfulness. One might argue convincingly that such a tendency is universal and always has been, but Americans have raised the tendency almost to the level of cult worship. The worship services themselves are not as shrill today as they were in the late 1960s, when being over thirty carried the kind of disenfranchisement that being under eighteen once had. Americans under the magic age flaunted their distrust of the older generation, and members of the older generation reacted either by returning the distrust or by affecting more youthful clothing, hairstyles, and manners of speech, and intoning that they didn't trust anyone over thirty either—except for themselves and a few close friends, of course. The world belonged to the Pepsi generation—as it always has—but this time the generation took its inheritance very seriously: to be young was to be wise; to be young was to be right. It was an old American dream: the dream of beginning all over again, with a fresh, youthful vision of truth. It was not just American, of course. Arthur had the dream, set up the Round Table, and with his knights carved some order out of chaos. But Arthur's court grew stale and the king himself grew old, and he made mistakes. It was young Percival, the pure, who saw the Grail.

Concomitant with our love of youth is our fear of aging. In its extreme forms this involves not just the very normal aversion to the infirmity of old age, but the simple dread of passing youth. It is a fear of maturity. Books on the midlife crisis, the middle-age doldrums, and the various "passages" of the post-thirty years flood the self-help sections of most bookstores. (Americans who grew up during the 1950s, 1960s, and early 1970s seem to be more introspective than Prince Hamlet; it has become almost fashionable now to wonder about one's own geriatric process.)

Another manifestation of our fascination with youth is our desperate fear of boredom. We demand change and novelty; the commonplace and routine are anathema. This is partly due to the relative wealth of our own society, an affluence that has made some sort of change possible for many Americans. It is also due to the relative safety of modern society; a measure of relief from boredom and sameness is found by challenging that very safety. There are some very real dangers in modern society, of course, ranging from personal assaults to automobile accidents and plane crashes, but the day-to-day business of living is predictably secure, even when it is hectic. Few people are in real danger of starvation or death by exposure, even in times when jobs are lost and work is hard to find, and for some, life is secure almost to the point of boredom. The challenges we choose are usually mannered and ritualistic; that is, they give the illusion of risk without the necessity of really incurring it. White-water rafting—in recent years a popular pastime—is an example of this ritualistic challenge to safety and the humdrum, providing the action and the illusion of real danger one might find on a roller coaster and doing it in a beautiful, natural environment.

A more disturbing manifestation of the frontier myth in our daily lives is our high regard for the flamboyant rebel. Americans will pay homage to practically any rebel so long as he is flamboyant enough and fairly young. Again, this is a universal human tendency rather than merely a national one, but our country's birth in rebellion just over two centuries ago, the frontier ethic, with its attendant emphasis on individualism, and the constant tension between the homogenizing forces of an industrial society and the heterogeneity of our population makes Americans more susceptible to rebel-worship than people in other societies might be. (It would be difficult to imagine, for example, the Japanese, with their homogeneous population and centuries-old tradition of supporting the state, becoming quite as enthusiastic about exemplary rebels as we are.)

The rebel-as-hero is a very old theme in Western society, going back at least as far as Aeschylus. (Earlier Greek writers mentioned Prometheus, but they did not give him the heroic dimensions that Aeschylus did.) Shelley's version of the Aeschylean hero was for the Romantic dissident the archetypal rebel against unjust authority. He is brave, self-sacrificing, immensely noble, and absolutely uncompromising. Blake and Byron also contributed to the ideal in the Romantic Period (though it could be argued that Byron's rebels, while as uncompromising and noble as any, are not much given to self-sacrifice). Fidel Castro and Ché Guevara were popular heroic figures on college campuses in this country just a few years ago; Castro still surfaces in that role from time to time. Observers who see the veneration of such heroes as evidence of communist leanings among the young are simply wrong; it is evidence instead of our natural tendency to look for flamboyant heroes who rebelled against a repressive authority. Whatever one thinks of Castro's politics, one must admit that he fits the popular requirement for the rebel-as-hero. He is striking in appearance, articulate, intelligent, and somewhat given to displays of flamboyance.

We tend often to persecute individual rebels who threaten or seem to threaten our most cherished institutions. We are not much less conservative than other societies have been in the attitudes we take regarding specific rebellious individuals, but we remain fascinated by their rebelliousness, and sometimes, after they are safely dead (or reformed), we make heroes of them. Our regard for the rebel has sometimes led us to glorify even destructive, self-seeking, evil figures like Luciano or Capone or Bonnie and Clyde as well as genuinely Promethean figures like Martin Luther King, Jr. On a more harmless level, we sometimes find heroism in any sort of maverick behavior, such as (in the South especially) bootlegging. (See Tom Wolfe's wonderful essay, "The Last American Hero," on the bootlegger/chicken farmer/racecar driver

Junior Johnson for one enthusiastic example.) In some circles, marijuana and cocaine trafficking has taken on just this kind of flashy attractiveness for those who are in search of a properly rebellious stance. Most people who are heavily involved in such smuggling are professional criminals whose business operations might also include the murder of competitors, but others are ordinary working people out to make a little money—or a lot of money—doing something that seems to them exciting and only minimally wrong. A few are simply thrill-seekers, seeing themselves and their confederates as dashing and adventurous rebels defying an unreasonable authority. For American moviegoers even heroic policemen are usually rebels and mavericks.[5]

We have glorified unlikely characters such as William Bonney (*Billy the Kid*) who probably was not even conscious of rebelling against anything, and who, according to the photographs we have of him, looked more like Mortimer Snerd than like Paul Newman, who once played a movie version of him. The James Dean figure—curled lip, surly, and brooding over some real or imagined wrong—is the Byronic hero gone to seed in a society that cannot understand the nobility of Byron's figure and so regards only his posing. The results are sometimes comical (as when huge crowds assemble to see Evel Knievel jump his motorcycle over something—over anything—and make him almost a cult figure, a flamboyant hero who defines himself only by risking more broken bones in the name of no cause except flamboyance). Sometimes the results are

---

[5] The dark side of the rebel-as-hero is the rebellious villain. An essay by Benjamin Stein suggests that one typical American mythic villain is the rural or small-town scoff-law, who is, in effect, the threatening twin of the sophisticated and enlightened urban adventurer. ("Whatever Happened to Small-Town America?" *The Public Interest* 44 [Summer 1976]: 17-26.) Stein says that urban-based movie and television script writers have effectively created this particular mythic villain—although one might argue that the polarization of the country during the early days of the civil rights movement also had a great deal to do with it. At any rate, one of the best popular examples was the movie *Easy Rider*, in which two pleasant, if somewhat vacuous, cocaine dealers (given to uttering sentences like, "It's O.K., man; you're doing your own thing.") are shotgunned all over a verdant Louisiana countryside by two rednecks in a pickup truck. After the carnage, the Byrds sing, "All they wanted was to be free. . . ."

simply bizarre, as when our need for heroes leads us to search for them among the Hell's Angels or the Blackstone Rangers.[6] We see charisma in rebellion, and we are a notoriously soft touch for any charismatic figure.

A final manifestation of our faith in the Myth of the New Beginning is the typically American belief that we can eventually find a solution to every problem. This is to say that we believe the new start—our national new beginning—counted for something, that it will work. We are Utopians, optimistic that one day (perhaps not a very distant day) will show us perfection.

One of the best discussions of this "millennialist" tendency in American thought is by Cleanth Brooks, R. W. B. Lewis, and Robert Penn Warren in an essay entitled "The Moderns: Founders and Beyond (1914-1945)."[7] American millennialism, say the authors, is typified by youthful enthusiasm and a knack for distorting reality: "Americans are prone to underestimate the recalcitrance of human nature and the untidiness of history."[8] Differences can be overcome; disagreements can be settled: only let us look at our problems logically and with an eye to a fresh solution. This is, of course, a laudable attitude in many ways. People who believe they can accomplish anything can, in fact, accomplish quite a lot. But our millennialism also has its darker aspects. It can make us unrealistically smug, secure in the confidence that we are right in our approach to problems. This is hypocrisy and self-righteousness, and it is precisely what many Europeans find so irritating about America and Americans. Former President Jimmy Carter, a quiet, sincere, soft-spoken gentleman, had a great deal of difficulty in getting along with some of the leaders of the European nations because they found him maddeningly

---

[6]The Blackstone Rangers became a *cause célebre* for a brief time in the 1960s when they were regarded as a black activist group fighting for the cause of civil rights. Detractors argued that they were, in fact, a mere street gang specializing in extortion, burglary, and robbery by force, but they wore jaunty berets and received some sympathetic press coverage from a hero-starved society.

[7]*American Literature: The Makers and the Making* (New York: St. Martins Press, 1973), pp. 1803-26.

[8]Ibid., p. 1824.

self-righteous. Mr. Carter knew what was moral, what was right; he had seen it in his own country. This is an unfair estimate of Carter's attitude, of course, but it is very much how he was sometimes *perceived* by some of our European friends. Furthermore, self-righteousness *per se* can be a dangerous and destructive force, even (perhaps especially) when it thinks of itself as working for the good of mankind:

> In American millennialism, one recognizes a great deal that is entirely admirable . No one is going to quarrel with the wish to abolish poverty, to see that children do not develop rickets from malnutrition, or that the aged have proper medical care. Nor is it less than noble to try to abolish war and to increase economic security and freedom for human beings throughout the world. . . . Nevertheless, there is another side to millennialism. . . . It is the arrogance of the fanatic who is willing to impose his judgments on other people because of his confidence that he knows the truth and that the erring brother will really be better off if forced to knuckle under.
>
> One turn of the screw and millennialism demands immediate solutions. Another turn of the screw and it demands whatever violent means may be necessary to achieve its solutions, for the ends can, for the millennialist, often be taken to sanctify the means. Thus, on this basis, communism and fascism may be considered to be violent and aggressive versions of millennialism, for though we tend to think of them as polar extremes, both show the tell-tale symptoms: a certainty of the possession of a privileged insight into the meaning of history and a fanatic determination to use that knowledge to set up the perfect society—along with a willingness to liquidate, if necessary, any opposers of the scheme.[9]

While the utopian tendency in this country has generally not been the cause of widespread bloodshed, it has in the past produced and continues now to produce various forms of repression. Although there was no widespread incarceration or liquidation of dissidents during the McCarthy era, as there might have been under a more totalitarian form of government, a growing fear of world communism as a threat to American ideals caused some very real wrongdoing.[10] People lost their jobs, their

---

[9]Ibid., pp. 1823-24.

[10]It is possible to see the flirtation that large numbers of American intellectuals carried on with Communism during the 1930s and afterwards as being a manifestation

reputations, and their friends, if not their lives or their liberty, and the threat of worse seemed real enough. There will always be, in any society, pressure from groups which believe themselves to be right, to have a corner on perception and morality. The pressure is always dangerous, whether it be from an established religious denomination or the Nazi Party or the Ku Klux Klan. Any group which believes itself in possession of Truth is capable of perpetrating any evil in the name of that Truth. A society's protection against such evil—the only real protection—is the ability to doubt the ultimate nature of any particular truth that is being foisted upon it.

Many popular books on do-it-yourself therapy draw heavily on what I have been referring to as the Myth of the New Beginning. Optimistic in tone, they stress the nearly limitless potential of every human being and urge us to accept ourselves, finally, as being only a little lower than the angels. Such optimism can make for creativity, but it has a curious potential for destructiveness as well. It is a fine thing to celebrate man's potential, but we must acknowledge his potential for limitless evil as well as for good. Man must understand what he can do in the way of evil before he can even pretend to be good. This is the beginning of morality, the psychological or spiritual or (in the present case) the mythical basis that makes morality possible.

One of the most moral (in this sense) books of the past century is Joseph Conrad's *Heart of Darkness,* because Conrad faces the problem of evil in man. He tells us that a man must recognize in himself the ability to put his enemy's head on a stick and dance around a fire with it, and only when he recognizes that potential can he even begin to deal with any moral problems at all. Some college students who have been nourished on pop psychology and told, "I'm O.K.; you're O.K." have trouble dealing

of American Utopianism growing out of a belief in the New Beginning. So steadfast was the belief in the efficacy of the New Beginning (in a Russian setting this time) that even rumors of the bloody purges at first could not shake it. Even after the Hungarian invasion in 1956, one could find a few sympathizers willing to overlook the Russian excesses, much as an observer sympathetic to the French revolution might have chosen to overlook the Reign of Terror. The dream still lived, even if men had bloodied it.

with Conrad; a few of them regard him as downright perverse. But if they are ever to become really educated adults with an ability to make important decisions for themselves and their world, they must deal with their capacity for evil. Nothing is more important in the long run. Germany could in part rationalize exterminating six million Jews because Germany thought that it was a moral country, that it was sophisticated. We can do absolutely anything if we forget even for a little while that we are capable of doing absolutely anything and so must not do it. The people who made Auschwitz and Belsen—and My Lai—possible were not madmen; they were decent fellows, just like us, who awoke one day to discover that they had become monsters.

Our faith in the Myth of the New Beginning is a source of vitality and creativity in America. It reflects a youthful ebullience of spirit, a ready determination to tackle any task that comes to hand, and it reflects a certain naiveté. Its only danger is that it can work to keep us from doubt and therefore from self-knowledge. We stand always—as all civilizations have stood—on the edge of barbarity, and it takes only the *hubristic* notion that we are immune to barbarity to push us over the edge. Our faith in the Myth of the New Beginning should not be a refuge from the hard truth that we, too, are susceptible, that we can be tragically, horribly wrong.

Chapter 5

Looking Outward:
The Myth of the State

> *The Prologues are over. It is a question, now,*
> *Of final belief. So, say that final belief*
> *Must be in a fiction. It is time to choose.*
> —WALLACE STEVENS

IN A 1940 POEM, "Asides on the Oboe," Wallace Stevens deals with the death of traditional mythic systems in modern society. Like many of Stevens's other poems, this one also brings up the question of the role of the artist or poet: to Stevens, he is the one man in all this disordered world who can make a new order. We see order reflected in art because it is the business of the artist to find or create order in the world.

Stevens says in the prologue (after having said that prologues are over) that our final belief comes down only to a matter of choosing among fictions. Stevens is never easy to discuss out of context, and the rest of the poem is relevant enough to the matter at hand to be quoted in its entirety:

I
That obsolete fiction of the wide river in
An empty land; the gods that Boucher killed;
And the metal heroes that time granulates—
The philosophers' man alone still walks in dew,
Still by the sea-side mutters milky lines
Concerning an immaculate imagery.

If you say on the hautboy man is not enough,
Can never stand as god, is ever wrong
In the end, however naked, tall, there is still
The impossible possible philosophers' man,
The man who has had the time to think enough,
The central man, the human globe, responsive
As a mirror with a voice, the man of glass,
Who in a million diamonds sums us up.

II

He is the transparence of the place in which
He is and in his poems we find peace.
He sets this peddler's pie and cries in summer,
The glass man, cold and numbered, dewily cries,
"Thou art not August unless I make thee so."
Clandestine steps upon imagined stairs
Climb through the night, because his cuckoos call.

III

One year, death and war prevented the jasmine scent
And the jasmine islands were bloody martyrdoms.
How was it then with the central man? Did we
Find peace? We found the sum of men. We found,
If we found the central evil, the central good.
We buried the fallen without jasmine crowns.
There was nothing he did not suffer, no; nor we
It was not as if the jasmine ever returned.
But we and the diamond globe at last were one.
We had always been partly one. It was as we came
To see him, that we were wholly one, as we heard
Him chanting for those buried in their blood,
In the jasmine haunted forests, that we knew
The glass man, without external reference.

The mythic system, complete with gods and heroes, that once made sense of the world for us is no longer available to us. Boucher de Perthes, a nineteenth-century French archaeologist whose work revealed man to himself (as a descendant of more primitive life forms) and so killed the gods forever, is typical of the forces which have shown our beliefs to be fictions. Now the most cherished fictions are obsolete, the statues of gods and heroes crumbling and rusting. There remains only "the impossible possible philosophers' man" for us to believe in; he is one last fiction—a fiction because he is not real, not one man ("impossible"), and yet worth our belief because he is potentially real ("possible"). His role is to show us to ourselves as well as sustain us. He is godlike, the only holy thing in a secular land (". . . alone still walks in dew"), and his words provide sustenance for a starving people (". . . by the sea-side mutters milky lines"). Unlike the crumbling metal statues of the dead myths, the images of the philosophers' man are "immaculate."

Even if our art, drawing on the myths of the past, says that man "is not enough"—that he is, though godlike ("naked, tall"), still only a man—we must look at what our philosophers' man will show us. He is the essence of what it means to be human, and as such, he reflects each of us, reveals us as we would be revealed in a mirror, only more deeply:

> . . . responsive
> As a mirror with a voice, the man of glass,
> Who in a million diamonds sums us up.

The poet, the artist, orders the world, and in his order we find peace. His is the voice that records or projects the sense of the world that any society must have in order to function coherently. He is "the transparence of the place in which / He is" because through him we see the order of things as they are. He names things—the month in summer called August, for instance—and in the naming makes them significant (makes them august, elevates them).

But in a world without gods, where men are, after all, only men and "ever wrong in the end," how does one deal with the facts of war and death? If the gods have a hand in such catastrophes as war, that is one thing; if some men are right and some are wrong in war, that is one thing; but if man "can never stand as god, is ever wrong / In the end, however naked, tall," that is quite another thing indeed. We are brought, then, to face man's fate without the illusions of the past that crowned or hid that fate, as flowers hide a bier. The scent of jasmine flowers is gone and we are left to ponder the stench of death.

Without illusions, without masking, heavily-scented flowers, we find "the sum of man." It is a hard thing, a painful thing, to have to grasp the world with such clarity—for us and for the man of glass: "There was nothing he did not suffer, no; nor we." Out of such suffering comes vision, if not comfort. Man is not a lesser god; he is not to be seen in terms of any divine prototypes. Man is only man; we must accept ourselves, must accept the vision of ourselves provided by the man of glass, without "external reference." He is us, the poet of only human life and death, the glass man through whom we see ourselves. We hear him mourning— "chanting for those buried in their blood"—for those buried only "in their blood," without jasmine crowns, and we have no need of gods' statues or holy books to decipher the song. The glass man's voice is not oracular; it is human.

We need not accept Stevens's vision of a secular universe ordered only by the artist-poet—after all, the prologue to the poem tells us that this vision, too, may be only one more fiction. Yet it is important to recognize the implications of the vision for modern myth-making. This humanistic-artistic approach to the problem of order in the world, while involving a hard acceptance of human limitations, also provides for a celebration of human dignity—a celebration because there can be such a thing as human dignity and human decency in the face of relentless and certain destruction. The ancient stoic philosophers in Greece understood this very well, but two thousand years of very non-stoical religious and philosophical tendencies since then have made the acceptance and the celebration difficult for moderns.

One reason the poet Robert Frost had such a difficult time with literary critics in the 1930s was that Frost, more so than most of his contemporaries, had an annoying tendency to insist on the limitations of human endeavor—even to glory in them. It was not enough that he said (along with dozens of other writers of the period) that man was not, after all, the apple in the eye of a paternal God and was therefore limited; Frost had to insist that man was further limited because he was essentially perverse, hardheaded, self-centered, and myopic, and that no amount of social reforms would help the situation very much. Liberal critics who were perfectly willing to see the gods killed off in the name of human progress were absolutely aghast at being told there was no such thing as human progress.

Frost had attacked a very highly cherished myth, or at least he seemed to have attacked it. He seemed to say that we must find consolation in our very transience, in the brave and stubborn struggle that is brave and stubborn precisely because it is doomed. He wastes no time with laments. Matthew Arnold did all the lamenting necessary in one wonderful poem called "Dover Beach." The speakers in Frost's poems address no mournful, cosmic last resorts. "Here it is," the poems say. "Isn't it fine and wonderful that human beings can live and flourish under such circumstances, even if they have to trick themselves a little bit in order to do it?"

In a seldom-anthologized poem called "Directive," Frost presents a powerful picture of man's limitations, a picture suggested by a fallen-down house in an abandoned New England town. The tone of the whole poem is chantlike, incantatory, from the opening lines to the final reference to a grail vision and a curious kind of salvation. The poem begins,

> Back out of all this now too much for us,
> Back in a time made simple by the loss
> Of detail, burned, dissolved, and broken off
> Like graveyard marble sculpture in the weather,
> There is a house that is no more a house
> Upon a farm that is no more a farm
> And in a town that is no more a town.

"Directive" gives us a picture of destruction that is very nearly absolute. In one section Frost describes a "belilaced cellar hole, / Now slowly closing like a dent in dough." The effect is of an apocalypse in miniature, and the sweet-smelling flowers do nothing to temper the terror. The conclusion is pure magic:

> Your destination and your destiny's
> A brook that was the water of the house,
> Cold as a spring as yet so near its source,
> Too lofty and original to rage.

(We know the valley streams that when aroused
Will leave their tatters hung on barb and thorn.)
I have kept hidden in the instep arch
Of an old cedar at the waterside
A broken drinking goblet like the Grail
Under a spell so the wrong ones can't find it,
So can't get saved, as Saint Mark says they mustn't.
(I stole the goblet from the children's playhouse.)
Here are your waters and your watering place.
Drink and be whole again beyond confusion.

Salvation here is through acceptance and understanding of human limitations; this acceptance and understanding lead to strength—even to celebration. The "wrong ones" are apparently those who would refuse to accept the scene for what it is, those who would soften it or evade the hard lesson there. We are invited to drink from the cold, calm waters of a brook "that was the water of the house"; we drink from the grail. And what is the grail vision? What are we granted as we take the cup? We are given sight of ourselves—our "destination and our destiny," Frost says. We are offered vision without illusion and it is a hard gift. There is no society around us to soften the gift or confuse us about what we are receiving: "Here are your waters and your watering place," the poet says. "Drink and be whole again beyond confusion."

But Frost, perhaps more than any other American writer, is the poet of the individual—one might almost say of the isolationist. Our need for community leads us to seek companionship, including a mythic vision that can be shared with others. If we can no longer find it in the form of church services or other significant religious observances, we will look for it elsewhere. As I noted in the last two chapters, The Myth of the New Beginning offers, for many Americans, a common ground of belief, no matter what form or expression the myth might take. There are dozens of other more or less tentative attempts to find a way of imposing meaning and order on experience. Most of these can be lumped roughly into two categories which I have chosen to call (for lack of better names), "Looking Outward" and "Looking Inward."

The tendency to turn outward in search of order and stability is a natural one in any society; it is, after all, the basis of religion. In America, the practice of turning outward to find significance predates the decay of the power of organized religion. The earliest settlers did not (as a rule) see themselves as Americans at all, but as transplanted Englishmen, and so they naturally judged their own lives in terms of European standards. Even years later, during America's colonial expansion when nationalism was at a fever pitch, the best books, the best food, the best music were, in the popular estimation, European. Emerson and Twain both scolded their countrymen for such slavish emulation, but the fact was that people in the young nation had a very real need for an external standard by which they could judge their own culture. The new American millionaires proudly pointed to American business and American railroads and American inventions, but they built their houses in imitation of the best European homes and imported their furniture from England, France, Italy, and Germany. Part of this, it is true, was simply a matter of snobbishness—of flaunting one's wealth and keeping up with the Vanderbilts—but quite a lot of it was also due to a deeply ingrained belief that European society was a mark against which one could be measured.[1]

The process of looking outward for a mythological tradition to replace or augment the ailing Judeo-Christian mythic structure, however, cannot properly be said to have begun in earnest until after the second decade of the twentieth century. By that time, Western man had begun to turn to a very great extent to areas other than religion in an attempt to deal with the question of meaning in life. (That is, men and women in large numbers, from diverse backgrounds, were turning to other areas. There had, of course, always been dissidents, skeptics, and other questioners, but never before on this scale.) The search led to the fields of government, biology, sociology, psychology, and—naturally—to philosophy. But philosophy was at this very crucial time divided sharply in

---

[1] The attitude persists in curious ways. In the minds of most American diners, the terms "fine food' and "continental cuisine" are synonyms—this despite the fact that those same diners would rather have a shrimp cocktail and a Kansas City steak than the continental cuisine.

several camps, and the most dominant voices in academic philosophy (those of the logical positivists) offered little solace and less direction for the man or woman wrestling with the *raison d'etre*. It was a virtue of that widely disparate group of writers and thinkers we now call the existentialists that it at least seemed more in touch with the problems peculiar to a modern industrial society than did most of the established academic philosophers.[2] However, the seemingly less cloistered, less bookish, more humane existentialists (who would become increasingly powerful in the next few decades) were only in agreement on the impossibility of turning to any exterior source for meaning.

The answer, in fact, came not from the ranks of the philosophers or the priests, but from the students of sociology and government. Turning outward in an attempt to find something larger than himself, something to which he could devote his energies and for which he could demonstrate the profundity of his belief, Western man discovered the Myth of the State.

There is nothing radically new in the kind of social fervor that goes to make up a state mythology. Ancient Rome certainly had a version of it; Romans even deified some of their emperors. One excellent historical discussion of the West's long-standing flirtation with a state mythology is Ernst Cassirer's classic, *The Myth of the State*. In this 1946 work, with memories of Germany's capitulation to the various myths that went to make up Nazism still fresh in his mind, Cassirer laments what he calls man's "primal stupidity" in allowing myth to take the place of rational thought. He fears the consequences if the powers of myth, including the Myth of the State, are not checked and subdued by superior forces: "As long as these forces, intellectual, ethical, and artistic, are in full strength, myth is tamed and subdued. But once they begin to lose their strength, chaos is come again. Mythical thought then starts to rise anew and to

---

[2]For a brief discussion of the impact of the existentialists on the community of academic philosophers, see F. H. Heinemann, *Existentialism and the Modern Predicament* (New York: Harper and Brothers, 1958).

pervade the whole of man's cultural and social life."[3] (Cassirer's view of myth as a dangerous and misleading falsehood is at odds with the attitudes of many mythologists who would tend to see mythology as a foundation of precisely the "intellectual, ethical, and artistic" forces Cassirer described.)

One of the most interesting examples of the Myth of the State—and one of its supreme instances—is to be found in the purest form of Marxism. What is so interesting here is the way in which a Myth of the State can so displace the previously established mythic patterns that it can become, in effect, a new religion—and one which (like many other new religions) tends to regard other traditions as deadly rivals. This is by no means to say that Karl Marx, working quietly in the British Museum in 1848, ever intended to establish anything like a religious movement. (Marx would have been horrified to think that anyone would link him with either religion or the state, for that matter; he saw himself standing in opposition to both.) He did want to do precisely what almost all religious writers have wanted to do, and that was to provide human beings with an understanding of their place in the world and their duty in it. In the industrialized nineteenth century, the Pauline doctrine of original sin and salvation did not make quite the tidy sense that perhaps it once had—or so it seemed to Marx. The key to an understanding of the human condition, he believed, was not natural depravity but economic determinism. He was a persuasive author and he found a receptive audience.

Marxism in its original form offers two powerful incentives to belief. The first is the millenarianist hope it holds for any oppressed and suffering people. In that way, first of all, it appeals in much the same way a religion might: things may be rough now, it says, but let us all work together and the future will be brighter. Furthermore, the brighter future is immediately at hand; one does not have to wait for another incarnation, a second coming of Christ, or a physical death and rebirth in order to reap

---

[3] *The Myth of the State* (New Haven and London: Yale University Press, 1946), p. 298.

the benefits. It is the second incentive, I believe, which largely accounts for the phenomenal attractiveness of Marxist philosophy in nations which are in the process of becoming industrialized. The possibility of every individual's taking part in initiating the new order, the millenarianist vision, is the attraction. No one is too poor, too humble, or too weak; the call to action is addressed to every believer. Men can live by almost any means, scratching a living out of poor soil or toiling day after day in factories, but men will live for—and die for, too, if they have to—the dignity that comes from seeing themselves as instruments of change for a better world. Anyone who would understand the attraction of Marxism in impoverished areas of the world must understand this very basic aspect of the human need for meaning, for order, and for dignity.[4]

While *The Communist Manifesto* is primarily a political argument, a call for revolution among the proletariat, it is not based merely on observations by Marx and Engels of the very real evils in nineteenth-century European society or on utopian dreaming. Rather, it is based on an outgrowth of Hegelian philosophy called (by Engels) dialectical materialism. Drawing heavily on Hegel's proposition that the essence of things is change, that every thesis must produce its antithesis, and that conflict will invariably lead to a synthesis of a new order, the new economic philosophy saw the proletariat revolution and the victory of communism as inevitable. That is, while the *Manifesto* itself can be seen as a mere call to arms (one of many at the time; all of Europe was in the throes of revolutionary fervor), it derives not from mere indignation but from an absolute conviction that the days of the bourgeoisie were numbered. Paul could not have been more convinced of the inevitability

---

[4]Of the quasi-religious attitude about the founders of world communism, Marx and Engels, Robert Heilbroner says, "If we are to judge by a count of worshipping noses, Marx must be considered a religious leader to rank with Christ or Mohammed, and Engels thus becomes a sort of Saint Paul or John. In the Marx-Engels Institute in Moscow, scholars have pored over their works with all the idolatry they ridicule in the antireligious museums down the street." See *The Worldly Philosophers: The Lives, Times, and Ideas of the Great Economic Thinkers*, 4th ed. (New York: Simon and Schuster, 1972), pp. 134 ff.

of the Second Coming than Marx was convinced of the inevitability of the
communist world state.

Now it is one thing to ask a man to give up what little security and
comfort he might have in order to support a revolution which might or
might not be successful. It is quite another to assure him that the victory
of the revolution is as inevitable and immutable as the natural laws that
govern the speed of falling objects or the expansion of gases, and
subsequently to offer him a chance to be part of the creation of a new
order that is sure to come. Marx offers exactly that assurance over and
over again in the *Manifesto*; victory is not just desirable—it is certain:

> The essential condition for the existence, and for the sway of the
> bourgeois class, is the formation and augmentation of capital; the condi-
> tion for capital is wage labor. Wage labor rests exclusively on competition
> between the laborers. The advance of industry, whose involuntary promo-
> ter is the bourgeoisie, replaces the isolation of the laborers, due to
> competition, by their revolutionary combination, due to association. The
> development of modern industry, therefore, cuts from under its feet the
> very foundation on which the bourgeoisie produces and appropriates
> products. What the bourgeoisie, therefore, produces, above all, is its own
> grave-diggers. Its fall and the victory of the proletariat are equally
> inevitable.

Not content with a mere assertion, Marx and Engels worked for
years on a mammoth, four-volume treatise called *Das Kapital*. Much of
the book is mere polemic and the argument sometimes gets lost in the
invective, but the essence of the work is a step-by-step explanation of the
inevitability of the victory of the system Marx had described in the
Manifesto.

One cannot help but notice a correspondence here between the
Marxist myth and the various utopian-paradisical myths of numerous
religions, including Christianity. As Mircea Eliade has pointed out, even
Marx's choice of words suggests a dependence on traditional eschatologi-
cal myths:

> Marx takes over and continues one of the great eschatological myths
> of the Asian Mediterranean world—the redeeming role of the Just (the
> "chosen," the "annointed," the "innocent"; in our day, the proletariat)

whose sufferings are destined to change the ontological status of the world. In fact, Marx's classless society and the consequent disappearance of historical tensions find their closest precedent in the myth of the Golden Age that many traditions put at the beginning and the end of history. Marx enriched this venerable myth by a whole Judeo-Christian messianic ideology: on the one hand, the prophetic role and soteriological function that he attributes to the proletariat; on the other, the final battle between Good and Evil, which is easily comparable to the apocalyptic battle between Christ and Antichrist, followed by the total victory of the former.[5]

Marxism as such received relatively little attention in the United States until well after the end of the First World War. There were serious efforts by socialists to make political headway (Eugene Debs ran for president on the Socialist ticket in 1912 and received nearly a million votes), but the socialists were, as a rule, a most non-militant group of idealists who liked to think of themselves as the intellectual descendants of Jefferson, Emerson, and Whitman. The seriously weakened economy of Europe—and the consequent disruption of the American economy in the great depression of 1929—forced Americans who might have flirted with socialist ideas previously to consider more drastic measures of reform. Marxism seemed to some an attractive alternative.

There are four reasons why Marxism attracted as many American intellectuals and writers as it did in the 1930s. The first and most obvious is the depression itself. It seemed to many that the means (capitalism) for bringing about the ideal American end (equality of opportunity— including, presumably, some measure of economic security) had completely broken down, and nothing less than a total restructuring of the system was necessary for the good of the entire population. There was a great deal of undirected dissatisfaction and general dismay at the sudden failure of an entire economic system. Confusion and desperation lead some to suicide or insanity and others to a determination to try virtually

[5]"Archaic Myth and Historical Man," *McCormick Quarterly* (January 1965): 21-22. Reprinted in Donald E. Hartsock, ed., *Contemporary Religious Issues* (Belmont CA: Wadsworth, 1978), p. 36. See also Raphael Patai, *Myth and Modern Man*, pp. 95-104, for a discussion of "The Myth of the Marxist World."

any remedy. In the 1930s, people who had read their Marx and Engels closely could point to specific sections of *Das Kapital* which seemed suddenly validated by the worldwide collapse of Western economies.

A second reason has to do with the egalitarian elements of the ideal Marxist state. Social and class distinctions would be abolished, any possibility of economic exploitation would cease to exist, and all men and women would be united in the common good.

A third and very potent reason for the appeal of Marxism at this time was its quasi-scientific rationale. Americans have always been impressed with any system that makes a show of appealing to scientific principles. After all, the country was, in a very real sense, a product of the Enlightenment. (See the discussion in chapter three.) Americans often show a willingness to place enormous faith in almost anyone who wears a laboratory smock and carries a clipboard. Marx, of course, did not have a smock, but he did have, with his neo-Hegelian view of history and economics, a decidedly no-nonsense aura of rationality, of scientific "rightness."

Finally, Marxism struck a resonant chord in its call for a new order—a new beginning. Few American myths are as deeply ingrained in the national psyche as the Myth of the New Beginning and communism seemed simply another version of it. (John Dos Passos said that Walt Whitman was at least as revolutionary as any Russian poet.) Americans *wanted* to see something new at work; some of them wanted it so badly that they could blithely ignore the imperfections, the breakdowns in the system which, in Russia, produced the terrible purges and grotesque enormity of human suffering. "I have seen the future," the American journalist and poet John Reed wrote, "and it works."[6]

---

[6]According to Brooks, et al., "Most American intellectuals did not become disillusioned with communism because of the contradictions in Marxist theory. They were disenchanted by particular events such as the pressure exerted on artists and intellectuals, the bloody purges carried out by Stalin, and, most notably, in 1939, the nonaggression pact signed by Hitler and Stalin which freed the Nazis to carry out their invasion of Poland, the overt act that opened the Second World War." See "The Moderns: Founders and Beyond," p. 184.

Marxism is only one means of focusing on *social* man—on human beings as they are affected by events outside themselves. For the true Marxist philosopher, to talk of subjective man is to talk gibberish, for human subjectivity is associated with bourgeois decadence. Marx saw human nature itself as being caught up in a vast, inexorable process. Human problems were, in the final analysis, social problems and they would be resolved with the destruction of the capitalist system. There is in pure Marxism a certain, curious optimism about human nature that stands in shocking contrast to the cynical, repressive regard for individual human beings in many Marxist states. Marx shows himself allied with the optimism of the Enlightenment by assuming that the only problems bothering man are external and temporary, and, once man is free to be the rational creature he was meant to be, all problems will vanish.

If communism is the most striking and extreme example of the tendency of modern man to embrace a Myth of the State, it is by no means the only example. Nazism and fascism, of course, have their own mythic overtones—as we can see by glancing at the course of events in Europe in the late 1930s and early 1940s. (For that matter, any political and economic system is capable of taking on mythic trappings. A whole body of mythic material surrounds such institutions as American isolationism, the "domino theory," free enterprise, and "rugged individualism"; much of this has already been commented on in chapter four.) Yet it is peculiar to Marxist communism that its ideology, its social theory, and even the language of its formative documents are all so heavily imbued with mythic elements (the chosen people, the trial, the apocalypse, the apotheosis of the hero—Lenin, for instance, or Marx himself—and the new Age of Gold) that it lends itself easily to people who are, whether they know it or not, anxious to find a coherent mythology.

Chapter 6

Looking Inward:
The Myth of the Self

> It's mighty
> peaceful on a raft.
> —Huck Finn

Anthropologists have found conclusive evidence that Neanderthal man, a subspecies that flourished for a while in Europe about the same time our own ancestors were getting a start there, had a system of beliefs which apparently involved ritual burial of the dead and the worship of some sort of deity—perhaps a bear-god, since skulls of cave bears have been found in piles with the artifacts of Neanderthal man. The last Neanderthal disappeared from the earth at least 35,000 years ago, quite possibly as a result of direct competition with early representatives of our own species. They grew no crops, raised no herd animals, and had nothing we would call a civilization. (The first settled communities that would produce real civilizations would not come for almost another 25,000 years.) Yet these people—and I think we must call them people, even though the scientific designation, *Homo Neanderthalis*, suggests something not quite, not fully human—worshiped a god and ritually buried their dead. They had a mythology—they must have had—perhaps a fully developed system of tales of heroes and supernatural agents, and the mythology (whatever it was, however unthinkably alien to our own) must have served the purpose of making sense of the world for them. They wondered about the world, and they looked for answers to their questions about the unknown, about life, fecundity, and birth, and of course about death. (We have evidence that they wondered about death.) In their wondering, they turned outside themselves. They looked for forces they imagined to be greater than themselves, forces that were outside the merely human world of change and death. That is a very human thing to do. It is an ancient pattern of human behavior, dating back at least to a time when near cousins of our own species, *Homo sapiens* (what a smug title!) displayed precisely the same pattern.

It would seem, then, that man has a natural tendency to look for something outside himself, something greater than himself, in which he can believe and to which he can devote some measure of his energies. If he is denied a belief in a specific metaphysical entity, he might merely replace the early belief with a more satisfactory one—one which more readily agrees with observable phenomena. If he finds himself in the position of having been denied belief in metaphysics altogether (as is sometimes the case in twentieth-century Western society), he might turn to a belief in something tangible, something physical but still much larger than the individual self in his search for meaning. A vision of the ideal republic, a Myth of the State, is one attractive alternative, and, as we saw in the preceeding chapter, it is a particularly effective one if it employs the imagery and the terminology of a metaphysical tradition. Another possible direction for the searcher disillusioned with his own mythic tradition is a completely foreign tradition, one he has not yet been forced (or has chosen not) to examine for failure to coincide with his other means of perception. In the United States, especially in the 1960s and 1970s, there was a tremendous growth in the popularity of several Eastern traditions, ranging from pure ascetic mysticism (the Hare Krishna cult) to the almost matter-of-fact (transcendental meditation). The popularity of classes in yoga and the various martial arts is due only in part to the fact that such disciplines provide recreation, excercise, and self-defense; part of the lure is the association with an exotic culture in which mystery and even magic still seem to have a part.

In the case of the more esoteric examples of Eastern mysticism, there is often a tendency to emphasize the nearly limitless potential of the individual—a potential which is to be tapped by following the regimen of the tradition in question. (This may be traceable in part to an imperfect understanding in the West of the philosophy of Zen which stresses the improvement of character through specific discipline.) So popularized, the Myth of the Inner Self holds that human beings possess an enormous amount of strength, energy, wisdom, or whatever—possess it in amounts that can only be called superhuman—and the key to fulfillment is learning how to tap those hidden and largely mysterious reserves. The process may involve special diets, meditation, exercise, or a special course of study. Now there is nothing wrong with any of the disciplines to which the American public often ascribes a degree of Eastern mystery; all of them, or variations of them, have been providing health, recreation, and physical and mental training, for many years, but few experts or serious practitioners of any of them would lay claim to powers which are in any way superhuman.[1]

The process of turning outward, beyond the self, in order to find a coherent mythic structure is a natural human tendency. Whether the result of that process is evangelical religion, mysticism, mythic nationalism, or a Myth of the State is immaterial; the process always derives from the common human need to perceive the self as a part of an ordered and coherent whole. In recent years, repeated frustration of efforts to find

---

[1]The persistent popularity in this country of films and television shows about mysterious figures who received training in esoteric disciplines and who possess virtually magical abilities as a result illustrates the desire to find magic in a scientific world and to believe in a hero with magical qualities.

Commenting on the popularity of Oriental traditions in general for Westerners, Kenneth Reagan Strunkel says that the "success of many 'gurus' in modern industrial states reflects at once the insecurity of values in the Occident and the fragmentation of India's great religious traditions." *Relations of Indian, Greek, and Christian Thought in Antiquity* (Washington DC: University Press of America, 1979), p. 152.

meaning outside the self has led Americans to discover (or rediscover—it is not entirely a new direction) the possibility of turning inward in search of structure. The methods used range from those of the scientist to those of the pure mystic. The result of the process, no matter what the methods, is a Myth of the Self; it is a formidable force in modern American society.

To European eyes, American society has always been marked by a certain sense of impermanence, a kind of restless and even willful instability. The thing that most impressed Charles Dickens on his first trip to the United States was the American practice of moving houses from one location in a city to another. House moving seemed to Dickens an awful metaphor for the general impermanence of the less tangible aspects of American society. The nineteenth-century French historian, traveler, and observer of manners, Alexis de Tocqueville, remarked that Americans, having (in their own minds, at least) severed ties with Europe and its past, seemed to have no sense of ever having had a past at all—as if the past were of no consequence. Even the awareness of family ties and relationships seemed insecure or of relatively minor importance: the peculiar American emphasis on individualism seemed to free every individual from a sense of the past. (I have never been able to discover if Henry Ford really said, "History is bunk." Whether he said it or not, the sentence comes very close to expressing sentiments he voiced on several occasions and it also comes close to expressing views shared by many of his countrymen. A professor of education once told me that he did not understand why school children were required to take "so much" history, when they needed to be developing an awareness of themselves as individuals.)

The critic and literary historian R. W. B. Lewis, writing about the tendency in American literature for the hero to isolate himself, both physically and psychologically, from the mainstream of society, once said that the process is so much a part of American fiction that it should be given a name—something like the "denitiation" of the protagonist, something appropriate to the reversal of the usual rites of initiation into society.[2] In fact, if we look at the protagonists of American fiction in the nineteenth and twentieth centuries, we find an enormous emphasis on withdrawal, isolation, and a certain, moody introspection.

Virtually all of Melville's major characters are (to use a term he invented to describe the crew of the *Pequod*) isolatoes. Faulkner's heroic figures turn their backs, figuratively or literally, or both, on society and try to come to terms with the universe on a very private level—Isaac McCaslin by renouncing and relinquishing his patrimony and paying off an old family debt, Bayard Satoris by refusing to live any longer by the rules of the "succinct and formal violence" of chivalry. Hemingway's characters are perhaps the most flamboyant in their renunciations of society and their need to find "a separate peace." (Hemingway nowhere makes this need more eloquently apparent than in the 1925 novel, *The Sun Also Rises*. An early scene in the novel shows Jake, an *emasculato*, watching Brett, an intensely sexual woman whom he loves but cannot have, dancing with a group of homosexuals, leaving Jake to make conversation with Georgette, a prostitute with bad teeth whom Jake has, with grim humor, introduced as his fiancee to a group of shallow dilettantes. One has only to contrast this nightmarish picture of a civilization turned upside down to the peaceful, overtly religious descriptions of the fishing in the mountains above Burgette, in Spain, to realize the truth in Lewis's statement that the proper rite of initiation, "given the character of society," is denitiation.[3])

It is not just the major writers or the almost major writers who reinforce and mirror for us this aspect of our culture, this tendency to escape from society and find meaning in some private, very personal way. We see it in our popular culture, in the perennial wandering gunfighters like Shane, or in the dozens of exciting versions of himself that John Wayne played during his movie-cowboy career. In other words, Americans have a deeply ingrained need to identify with the hero who simply

---

[2]R.W.B. Lewis, *The American Adam: Innocence, Tragedy, and Tradition in the Nineteenth Century* (Chicago: University of Chicago Press, 1955), p. 117.

[3]Ibid.

turns his back on society—perhaps because they share his belief that society may, in the final analysis, be irredeemable. Some of the reasons for this ready identification with the hero-as-rebel were discussed in the fourth chapter, the one dealing with the Myth of the New Beginning. Another reason has to do with a peculiarly American brand of philosophy called pragmatism.

It was William James who gave the term pragmatism currency, but it was not his term; he borrowed it from his flamboyant fellow philosopher, Charles S. Peirce. I said the philosophy is peculiarly American because it seems a natural offshoot of our confident materialism. It holds simply that the meaning of any course of action is determined by the observable consequences; the course of action has no meaning apart from those consequences. Theories, ideals, precedents—all these are insignificant in the face of the measurable result of the chosen course of action. It is only natural that a country born at the height of the Age of Reason and coming into power in the early nineteenth century as a leader in all things having to do with technology should come up with a philosophy like pragmatism. In all American literature, there is no better example of a pragmatist than Huckleberry Finn.

Huck finds it necessary to explain over and over again, especially in the early chapters of the novel, that he has trouble following the course prescribed by the religion of the Widow Douglas because he was not "brung up to it." The widow is an idealist; she is a kind, moral, loving woman who thinks and acts by preconceived standards. Huck sees all this as signs of "respectability," and he needs to feel a part of her world while he lives in her home, so he tries to adapt his thinking to her idealism. But it doesn't work for him. He has no use for the story of "Moses and the Bulrushers" because Moses is dead and therefore of no importance to anyone. Huck brands Tom Sawyer's elaborate robber-baron fantasies as having "all the marks of a Sunday School." The closest thing to a religion Huck has is his superstition, which is for him a more practical approach to the unknown than orthodoxy can provide. Superstition, at least, provides for Huck omens of dangers to come; he is unable to get anything but platitudes from religion. His moral consciousness (as opposed to the "deformed conscience" inflicted on him by society's training) is based on this pragmatic attitude. Unrestricted by the limitations of an idealistic moral code, this consciousness can grow in association with the escaped slave, Jim; pragmatism allows for that kind of growth in the face of the unexpected, but idealism does not.

The first real battle between the conscience implanted in Huck by the religious training of the widow's respectable society and his growing sense of personal involvement with Jim takes place in chapter sixteen of the novel. Huck succumbs for a little while to the pangs of his conscience and decides to hand Jim over to the authorities. Confronted suddenly by the realization of the man's dependence on him and loyalty to him, he wavers in his resolution. When he is forced by the two men in the skiff to choose between what his conscience tells him is right and his loyalty to Jim, he hesitates a moment, then rejects his "respectable training."

The scene marks the beginning of Huck's pragmatic morality, for he justifies his action in a manner completely foreign to the approved morality of the society which he has fled. He decides that he will determine the advisability of any course of action in the future by its convenience and by the way it will make him feel afterwards. His action in remaining loyal to Jim produces mixed feelings of guilt and relief, but he realizes that the opposite course of action would also have produced mixed feelings. No fixed moral code weighs the scale in either direction. The wages of what society calls evil and the wages of what it calls good are the same, and Huck makes the reasonable and entirely practical resolution to "do whichever come handiest at the time."

The most dramatic split between the widow's idealism and Huck's pragmatism comes when Huck makes his final decision to help Jim even at the cost of his own soul. The struggle clearly is between the conscience that society, with its religious platitudes and its rigid formulas, has imposed on him and the pragmatic moral sense he has developed during his close association with Jim. To see Huck as an effective moral agent, we must see him in sharp contrast, not only to such self-seeking characters as

Miss Watson and the King and the Duke but to kindly Widow Douglas as well. The widow is an aristocrat and a respectable member of a slaveholding society, and we must assume that she not only supports slavery as an institution but would be truly horrified by Huck's abolitionist tendencies. In this respect she is much like the description Mark Twain once gave of his own mother:

> We lived in a slaveholding community; indeed, when slavery perished, my mother had been in daily touch with it for sixty years. Yet, kind-hearted and compassionate as she was, I think she was not conscious that slavery was a bald, grotesque and unwarrantable usurpation. She had never heard it assailed in any pulpit but had heard it defended and sanctified in a thousand; her ears were familiar with Bible texts that approved it but if there were any that disapproved it they had not been quoted by her pastors; as far as her experience went, the wise and the good and the holy were unanimous in the conviction that slavery was right, righteous, sacred, the peculiar pet of the Deity and a condition which the slave himself ought to be daily and nightly thankful for. Manifestly, training and association can accomplish strange miracles.[4]

The Widow is a very moral-minded aristocrat, capable of numerous acts of kindness, but her charity, unlike Huck's, is confined to the limits of her socially recognized ideals. Her ready-made ethical code, her idealistic notions about good and evil, are applicable only in limited circumstances. We learn later that she had tried to dissuade Miss Watson from selling Jim down the river, but she would never have argued for his freedom—much less steal him. Huck substitutes for her idealism a moral view that is void of ideology, one that is capable of operating outside the confines of society.

The problem is, according to Twain, any code of morality which has its roots in idealism is likely to be ineffective; idealistic morality is capable of true good only when the good that it causes corresponds with the established ideals. (Miss Watson's morality, by the way, is merely an ironic perversion of this idealism, and it is only intended to benefit her

---

[4]*The Autobiography of Mark Twain*, ed. Charles Neider (New York: Harper and Row, 1959), p. 30.

personally. She is as much a sham as the King or the Duke.) Huck Finn's pragmatic view of morality, which ignores ideals altogether, determines whether an action is good or bad by evaluating the probable results of the action. As long as he is on the river and away from the corruption of society (especially in the comic but sinister form of Tom Sawyer), he is able to live according to this pragmatic code of ethics. What makes the book the darkly powerful and disturbing work it is, however, is the boy's inability to live by this code once he is back in society. Once back in the clutches of Tom Sawyer, Huck rearranges his world to give it the order and coherency it needs. In this sense, at least, Twain's most famous story is a tragedy dealing with Huck's inabilities (and our own; who among us is purer than Huck Finn?) to supersede the mythic structure that our societies impose.

The flight from society to the self does not always entail the formulation of a new moral ethic. It might simply be a running away from any kind of responsibility. There is also the possibility of Byronic wandering—flight from what seems the dull, sheeplike, pointless life of society to a more vigorous, exciting life in a world that seems newly centered around one's own ego. This is an extremely tempting form of escapism, but it suffers from a lack of credibility when one tries to build a structure around it. This is because it demands the elevation of the ego to a level that most people over the age of seventeen find preposterous (or—far worse—simply funny). Gods and devils can get by with such posing in epics; even mortal Byron could pull it off once in a while. But the creation of a personality so powerful and dark and brooding and singular that it creates a world apart, a world with different rules and a different order, demands the suspension of more disbelief than most modern readers are willing to suspend. In fact, the Byronic hero never really caught on in America, perhaps because of competition with other flamboyant but less complicated rebels. There is an element of Byronism, of course, in Melville's brooding titan, Ahab, but *Moby Dick* is not "about" Ahab himself in the way that *Childe Harold's Pilgrimage* is "about" Harold. Ayn Rand attempted the creation of several Byronic outsiders, but most readers find the characters a little embarrassing. In American literature, at least, the *ubermensch* (by whatever name) has not been a very important figure.

There is another form of return to the self, one that seeks not to establish differences between the individual in question and society in general so much as to recognize and explore the commonality of a specific experience—the experience of having lost a belief in the myths, the order, that once made life (in or out of society) worth living. It is no accident, I think, that Freudian psychology caught on as something of a fad in the years following the First World War. The sense of the loss of order, of meaning, in the 1920s was general, and the new science of psychology gave people who were interested in discussing the problem of existence some basis for discussion. This new psychology made possible the consideration of man and of man's behavior from an entirely new point of view, one radically different from that of the theologian and somewhat more interesting than that of the biologist. When Shakespeare had Hamlet pose the question, "What a piece of work is a man?" the prince was able to answer it himself in terms of the accepted theological and philosophical constructs of the day, and the answer still left room for Hamlet's own individual problem. But when the question is asked in the twentieth century, the petititioner must be ready to qualify his question: Does he mean man as a social animal? Man as an organism? Man as a product of his environment? Man as a complex psychological being? Or man (and here one hesitates; the ground seems unsure) as a moral agent? The question is harder now.

Psychology came along, in a sense, at just the right time. It was very much needed—human behavior was just as complex as it had ever been, but some of the old ways of evaluating that behavior had apparently lost their validity. That is to say, psychology (along with other social sciences such as sociology and anthropology) made possible the consideration of man as a natural rather than primarily a metaphysical phenomenon, which in turn meant that not only man's respiration, blood flow, and body chemistry but also his attitudes, behavior, and patterns of belief could be looked at objectively and scientifically.

Carl Jung explained, in an essay called "The Modern Spiritual Problem," that modern man no longer feels as if religion were something welling up within himself—that it is instead something imposed from without, the way the strictures of any other institution are imposed from without. The various forms of religion, then, no longer appear "to be expressions of his own psychic life; for they are to be classed with the things of the outer world. He is vouchsafed no revelation of a spirit that is not of this world; but he tries on a number of religions and convictions as if they were Sunday attire, only to lay them aside again like worn-out clothes."[5] The urge for some sort of spiritual order, said Jung, arises from the depths of the human psyche, but the old religious forms no longer can be counted on to give it proper expression: "The passionate interest in these movements [that is, various religious and quasi-religious movements ranging from occultism to Christian Science—all of them attempts to revivify flagging religious attitudes] arises undoubtedly from psychic energy which can no longer be invested in obsolete forms of religion."[6] (Jung said elsewhere that most of the patients he had treated had been Protestants, with a few Jews, and a much smaller number of Catholics. Virtually all of them had come to him because, in the deepest sense, they had lost "a religious outlook on life." "It is safe to say," he continues, "that every one of them fell ill because he had lost that which the living religions of every age have given to their followers, and none of them has been really healed who did not regain his religious outlook. This of course has nothing whatever to do with a particular creed or membership of a church."[7])

Despite their idealization of rugged individualism, Americans, like people in every other society, have always exhibited a need to feel a part of

---

[5]Collected, with other essays in C. J. Jung, *Modern Man in Search of a Soul*, trans. and ed. W. S. Dell and Cary F. Baynes (New York: Harcourt, Brace and Company, n.d.), pp. 196-220.

[6]Ibid., p. 207.

[7]See "Psychotherapists or the Clergy," *Modern Man in Search of a Soul*, pp. 221-44.

some system of order, some meaningful pattern of existence that would in turn give their individual lives meaning. If they suffered from a discontinuity that rendered them unable to feel a part of historical events in the lands from which they came, they still had a very human need to belong to something. In the twentieth century, in the absence of an accepted metaphysical tradition, this sometimes took the form of a need to belong to a particular social or political group. The new left movement of the 1960s played the very important role of providing a kind of haven for believers—or, to be more accurate, for people with a very strong need to believe but with an acute awareness of the loss of belief in traditional American myths. During the height of this period, young people were very rapidly abandoning the system of beliefs and the codes of behavior built on those beliefs held by their parents' generation. But, since human nature abhors a vacuum, they found it necessary to erect a new system of beliefs and to cling to it with at least as much vehemence as earlier generations had to theirs. The youth-oriented music, cinema, and drama of the late 1960s were expressions, not simply of the rejection of an outdated order, but of the celebration of an entirely new order. (One exemplary version of the Alleluiah Chorus was "The Age of Aquarius.")

The United States, having found its strength first as a leader in technology, has always placed a premium on machinery—not just physical machinery, but the machinery of politics and social action as well. However, some problems stubbornly defy the best machinery, even that which seems (like the elevated mortals Euhemerus mentioned) completely divine. The best machines are human in their design, and they are flawed. The Age of Aquarius was just one more period, one more decade or so, after all.

The general loss of faith in the optimistic schemes of the new left had a profound effect in the 1970s. There followed a distrust of political movements, a tendency to avoid commitment to any sort of ideology. Pollsters sometimes mistook this tendency for mere apathy, but it was something far different. It was a reaction, not unlike a cry of pain, to the loss of belief in a structure that had, for a little while and for a whole generation, made sense of the world. In one of the best examinations of the life of the 1970s, Christopher Lasch points to the experiences of disillusioned new left leaders themselves. They moved, Lasch explains, toward a kind of narcissism that characterizes the whole post-new left period. Rennie Davis, having left radicalism to embrace what Lasch calls "the therapeutic sensibility," became a follower of the teenage guru, Maharaj Ji. Abbie Hoffman decided that the most important thing was "to get his own head together." Jerry Rubin, "having reached the dreaded age of thirty and having found himself face-to-face with his own private fears and anxieties, moves from New York to San Francisco, where he shops voraciously—on an apparently inexhaustible income—in the spiritual supermarkets of the West Coast."[8] (Rubin took what he calls a "journey into myself" that involved est, gestalt therapy, bioenergetics, rolfing, massage, jogging, health foods, tai chi, Esalen, hypnotism, modern dance, meditation, Silva Mind Control, Arica, acupuncture, sex therapy, Reichian therapy, and More House—a smorgasbord course in New Consciousness."[9])

For those who had rejected older traditions for the ideology of new left radicalism, the apparent bankruptcy of that ideology left a disturbing void. There now suddenly seemed to be a complete lack of exterior forms, of lasting institutions or traditions of which the individual could feel a part. Christopher Lasch says that one result of this sudden undermining of the secure ground of belief was the rise of the cult of the expert. No longer confident in their abilities to make important decisions for themselves, Americans turned to experts to make their decisions for them. Every big-city telephone directory lists experts on decision making, on child rearing, on career planning, on personal awareness, on sex, on everything. Another result was the desire to turn inwards, to find a private peace within the self, since it seemed that only the self could be either known or trusted.

---

[8] *The Culture of Narcissism: American Life in an Age of Diminishing Expectations* (New York: Norton, 1979).

[9] Ibid., p. 14.

There are three reasons for the increased emphasis on the self and on the power of the individual. The first lies in the egalitarian idealism which is associated with the nation's founding and which forms an important part of a residual American mythology. American idealists want to believe in the potential of every individual; new theories in education even suggest that it is unnecessary for any child ever to experience failure in his academic career. The rags-to-riches American success story is only a metaphor, set in materialistic terms, for a profound and pervasive belief in the nearly limitless potential of every individual. A very sophisticated, intelligent European friend who had spent years in Africa tried recently to explain to me what he saw as innate differences among various tribes. Some of these were cultural differences, but some were differences of character—which is to say, differences in potential. It struck me as a very unAmerican thing to say: that is, unAmerican in the sense that it conflicted with the idealistic belief in human potential.

A second reason for the increased emphasis on the self is the natural reaction to the profound sense of isolation that the individual feels in a relatively rootless, discontinuous society. Unable to feel a part of any meaningful exterior entity, he asserts his own power and his own validity. The reaction is very much like the adolescent tendency to regard the self as perfect in some areas—blessed, for instance, with an absolute corner on sensibility and perception. No one else feels the way he does; no one else understands the way he does. He is unique. Of course the world misunderstands him because the world is not as capable as he of understanding on any level. Most adolescents go through this stage; it is a perfectly natural reaction to the awful fear of imperfection, and not "measuring up," and to the knowledge that he does not yet quite fit into the adult world he sees around him.

A third reason for the rise of a cult of the self is the emphasis in psychoanalysis and other forms of therapy on "confronting" all aspects of one's personality—one's desires, dislikes, fears, aversions, attractions, whims—and nourishing them because they make the self unique. We "get to know" ourselves, we "explore" our own potentials and personalities, and by so doing we recognize at once our own uniqueness and the commonality of our need.

In the past (and to a certain extent even now) the cult of the self was usually considered to be a phenomenon of the rich, especially the rich with the added luxury of time on their hands. People worried about their ability to feed their families, or fearful that their furniture will be repossessed, or concerned that a combination of high interest rates and restricted employment possibilities may make impossible the dream of owning a home—or even renting a decent one—have more than their share of problems but the nagging worry that they are unfulfilled as human beings, that their lives are empty merely because they are not realizing their full potential, is not very high on the list. Furthermore, the rich have the time and the money for therapy—an enormously expensive remedy for the *angst* of the modern world—and they frequently find that the therapeutic approach which emphasizes their uniqueness and encourages them to "accept themselves as OK" increases their feeling of isolation, of dead-endness. They have nothing to work for except the aggrandizement of their own self-image, and this is not enough, because they are invariably driven to realize that the individual self is limited. It grows old; it breaks down, it is not any longer (if it ever was) the center of anyone else's attention; it is a lonely self because it does not belong to anything, does not believe in anything, and does not take joy in anything except its own reflection in the eyes of other people. *"L'enfer c'est les autres,"* said a character in Sartre's *Huis Clos;* one might add, "especially when they don't notice."

The pervasive feeling of emptiness and meaninglessness that drives those who can afford it to the couches of their analysts is no longer a phenomenon merely of the wealthy. The middle-income worker and the poor share the general anxiety, the restlessness, that once marked the complaints of the moneyed few. This is due partly to the general dissemination of information about expectations and self-fulfillment, a dissemination that takes varying forms, from greater educational opportunities to the popularization and increased availability of therapeutic counseling. But a much larger factor is the spread of dissatisfaction with traditional patterns of belief. It has become increasingly difficult for Americans on many levels to embrace belief in the efficacy of religion, of politics, of social action, and of virtually everything else ouside the self. They are driven, then, back to a reliance on the self, but often it is not a healthy self-reliance, not the rugged individualism of American mythology or the healthy skepticism of Emersonian philosophy, but a brooding, desperate, narcissistic preoccupation, a self-absorption and self-contemplation that only increases their already stark loneliness. They are not skeptical but cynical, not individualistic but merely isolated.

What one sees in this country now, on many levels, is profuse evidence of the loss of belief in external forms of all kinds. Perfectly rational people talk in perfectly rational tones about the breakup of civilization, about taking to the woods and growing a garden and arming themselves to keep away starving neighbors and other thieves, about armageddon, civil strife, the apocalypse. (A survivalist in Arkansas told a friend of mine that the true test of survivalist mentality was not whether you were willing to kill your neighbor to keep him from stealing your cow, but whether you were willing to kill the neighbor in order to get *his* cow.) Intelligent people with an ability to recognize empty rhetoric and a distaste for clichés talk very seriously about "getting their heads together" and "recognizing the child and the parent" within themselves and "finding true inner peace." There is no easy cure; perhaps there is no cure at all. In an effort to find meaning in their lives, sufferers might try anything from delusional fantasies of invincibility (the survivalist) to mind-expanding drugs to a wide variety of sexual roles and experiences to encounter therapy. Any of these might relieve the symptoms, and to that extent they are beneficial; but the loss of belief in the validity of life, in the *meaning* of individual life, is not likely to be cured by either recreation or fantasy or counseling. Mythology, when it works, provides a sense of that validity and that meaning. When it does not work, when it becomes merely a collection of tales without the immediacy of truth, a society must then seek meaning in other ways and with other myths. Whether the myth of the self can provide that meaning for Americans remains to be seen.

Chapter 7

Myth and Order

Do you see that cloud
that's almost in shape
like a camel?
—HAMLET

W E MIGHT THINK OF A mythic system as a kind of filter through which information must pass. In the process, it becomes ordered and coherent. If the filter were suddenly to be removed, the information would crowd in on the mind in a confused jumble, and the mind would be overwhelmed and rendered momentarily helpless by the onslaught of disordered perception. While the external conditions might be no more complex or disorderly than they were before, the mind, suddenly buried in an avalanche of stimuli, would see only chaos. The breakdown of a mythological system must occasion widespread confusion and chaotic conditions as a society tries to find a way of making sense of the world.

This is precisely what happens when a traditional, very non-Western society finds itself launched precipitously into the conditions of the modern, Western world. Some of the emergent nations of sub-Saharan Africa are good examples. If we look at the various tribes of the Bantu linguistic group scattered across central and southern Africa, we find a people who, less than a century ago, were living in conditions very closely resembling those of the tribes of northern Europe at about the time Julius Caesar sent his legions there. In fact, as Lewis H. Gann has pointed out, the inhabitants of this part of Africa have experienced, often in the course of a single lifetime, a degree of change that is staggering to contemplate:

> A hypothetical Ngoni born in 1880 would have been brought up under conditions comparable in certain respects to those of the Teutons in Roman times as described by Tacitus. He would have marched to war against the British in 1898, with his spear, his knobkerrie, and his great oxhide shield. He would have experienced defeat at the hands of the invaders; he would have witnessed the appearance of new industrial marvels—steam engines, motor trucks, and jet planes. One of his sons might have become a factory worker in Bulawayo; a second, a welfare officer in Mufulira; a third, a secondary schoolmaster in Ndola; and a fourth, a prominent politician. As an octogenarian, the Ngoni veteran might have been sufficiently hale and hearty to attend his country's independence celebration in 1964.[1]

These far-reaching and dramatic changes in the obvious, external circumstances of a hypothetical African are impressive in themselves, but the impact of such changes on the mythic system—and hence on the mind itself—is devastating. The Bantu tribes had a complex mythology which had made sense of the world for them for thousands of years. Western man has always entertained the unfortunate notion that the religious traditions of other societies were childlike and unrealistic. This is, of course, a foolishly myopic attitude; Bantu religious beliefs are not demonstrably more childlike or less realistic than the beliefs of either Christians or Jews. They simply assume and depict a completely different, a radically non-Western world view. The difficulty comes, here as in any tradition, when the tales which reinforce or demonstrate that world view no longer are in accordance with observable phenomena. It is as if those Teutonic tribesmen Tacitus observed in the first century B.C. had, between the beginning of the reign of Julius Caesar and the end of the reign of his successor, Augustus, witnessed the turmoil attendant on the

---

[1]*Central Africa: The Former British States* (Englewood Cliffs NJ: Prentice-Hall, 1971), pp. 285-86.

trial of Galileo; the discovery of the New World; the change from nomadic wandering to the feudal system to monarchy to parliamentary democracy; and from subsistence farming, hunting, and gathering to industrialization; the Newtonian universe; the Darwinian theory of evolution; the machine age; the jet age; and the atomic age. Tales and traditions that made the world sensible and orderly, that fit all or nearly all observable phenomena in 1880, were wildly in contradiction to observable phenomena in 1980. The predictable result was disassociation, as the African tried bravely and resourcefully, as all men will, to live in the world and be a part of it.

A single specific example illustrates what can happen when one is forced suddenly to leave behind—at least superficially—a complex and comprehensive mythic system based on extended family relationships. The Shona tribes of Zimbabwe, like all or almost all Bantu groups, have a complicated pantheon of ancestral spirits and tribal spirits who are intimately involved with the affairs of ordinary mortals. The creator figure, called *Musikavanhu* (from *musika,* "to create," and *vanhu,* "human beings") is completely detached from the day-to-day affairs of the mortal world.[2] More accessible is the *mhondoro,* or chief tribal spirit, whose advice is sought on matters of importance to the community as a whole and whose agent in this world is the chief. The chief is able to communicate with the *mhondoro* through a medium—often a sister or a niece. Most accessible and immediately important are the *vadzimu* (plural; the singular is *mudzimu),* the ancestral spirits.

An important link between the mortal world and the spirit world is the *nanga,* or herbalist. (The term witchdoctor has misleading connotations; it is part of the business of the *nanga* to expose for punishment practitioners of witchcraft. The *nangas* are primarily healers, advisers, and diviners of fortunes; virtually all of them claim supernatural powers.) The *nanga* is in nearly constant contact with the ancestral spirits, and he serves as a bonding agent who holds together the entire family unit—not

---

[2]I am indebted to Rolv Lind of Richmond, Virginia, and to A. C. Hodza of the University of Zimbabwe for information on Shona religion.

just the immediate family but the extended family and not just the living members but the dead ones as well. Family duties are tremendously important; a man who falls on hard times has the right to be fed and housed by his more fortunate relatives for almost any length of time. The family has a sacred obligation to look after all its members, and this obligation is so strong that it extends even to family members who have died. Pots of beer are placed outside villages in the darkness so the *vadzimu* can drink their fill, and if the beer is untouched the next day, the *nanga* is consulted to find out what has offended the ancestral spirit.

The extended family obligations, the omnipresence of the *vadzimu*, and the law-giving nature of the *mhondoro*—which can be seen as a kind of chief ancestral spirit, since the tribe itself resembles a greatly extended family unit—all made for a cohesive and comprehensible social structure that was reinforced by every aspect of the traditional religion. The entire system made sense of the world and agreed nicely with observable phenomena for thousands of years. Suddenly, however, it is required to operate in a completely foreign context, the context of parliamentary democracy or of some other twentieth-century notion of how society should run. Observers from the Western democracies are critical: "You have staffed your cabinet with members of your own family. You have made your brothers and cousins your deputy ministers. This is nepotism." Nepotism it may be, but it arises not out of avarice but out of concern for family reinforced by untold centuries of religious precepts demanding just this sort of thing. To do anything less would be shameful; it would be wrong.

"You are favoring your own family and your own tribe at the expense of others," the observer says. "This is not true democracy; all must take part in the law-making process." But the *mhondoro* is the giver of laws, and every facet of a religion at least as old as Christianity supports the chief of a tribe as the earthly agent of the *mhondoro's* laws. If a conflict exists between the law given by the *mhondoro* and the wishes of another tribe, that is simply unfortunate. Doubtless a compromise can be worked out, but until then, problems will exist.

The Western observer throws up his hands in despair; he wonders how people can be so blind to the logic of parliamentary democracy. But in fact that is not the real wonder at all. The marvelous thing is that they can make it work, that they can develop on a nationwide scale a system of government while at the same time holding on to a mythic system that originated in and only works smoothly with a society composed of readily identifiable extended family units. There are occasional tragic and bloody failures, of course, such as that in Uganda under Idi Amin, but the African states certainly have no monopoly on failed attempts at democracy. That some states have achieved a high degree of stability and prosperity in such a short time is a remarkable monument to the human ability to deal with the most radical and disturbing kind of change.

A change in the mythic structure is invariably a catastrophic change for society because the mythic structure is, in the final analysis, the way the society imposes order on the world. We can see this easily by examining other societies or by looking at their history or our own, but we cannot as readily identify the always fragile structures by which we live. We are too close to them. It is difficult to get a good answer to the questions, "What myths do you live by; what system of imposing order on the world do you habitually use?" because most people do not think of mythology except as a curio, a piece of antiquity outgrown by a mythless age. Baldyr is slain by the mistletoe. Phaedra is driven mad by the power of a remorseless Aphrodite. Prometheus steals the fire of Zeus and makes civilization possible. The tales are mementos of the past, faded but still interesting pictures of our ancestors and their quaint beliefs.

In the last analysis, we see what we must see, not what is. Our picture of the world is just that—a picture. This is true of little things, of our understanding of single phenomena like the nature of grass or of leaves. We tend to describe these things in terms first of all of their color, then perhaps of their shape and size, then in other ways. There are aspects of the phenomenon that we would not use in our description at all because we would not perceive those aspects. The grass would look—it would be—very different if we saw a little further up the spectrum of light, in ultraviolet, perhaps, or a little further down, in infrared. It would be the same grass or leaves, yet it would impinge upon our world in a very different manner, and so our picture of it would be a different picture.

If this is true of little things like the look of grass or leaves, it is also true of larger things such as our understanding of our relationship to the whole world of phenomena. It is characteristic of human beings that they must see themselves as having some sort of relationship to the goings-on of the universe, whether that imagined relationship takes the form of a projected ideal state or a kinship with the Creator himself. The organized attempts of men and women to wonder about the world are called science, philosophy, religion, and mythology. Mythology is simply the system of tales and stories in which some of the results of a society's wondering are expressed.

It is interesting that many people who cannot distinguish the colors red and green live out their lives assuming that they see exactly the same world that other people see. Their world is subtly different from yours and mine; it is recognizably the same world, but it is different enough so that one part of our way of seeing, of giving order to the world, is to them meaningless. It is perhaps only a little more difficult for a color-blind person to imagine red and green than it is for a person firmly rooted in one mythological tradition to see the world as it appears to his distant neighbor with a radically different system of order. But it is worth the effort.

We might extend this idea of different perceptions by analogy. Imagine for a moment two people standing side-by-side in a field at night, looking up at the sky. Now, there is nothing more objective than a night sky since there are exactly so many stars in exactly so many places. At the same time, nothing is more subjective than a night sky because the panorama of stars is essentially random and meaningless until our perception orders it and creates meaningful patterns. The two observers will see the patterns differently, and the difference might not be as subtle as the difference between the way we see a tree and the way our color-blind friend sees it. They would, naturally, see the same sky, and if a third person could draw the scene, both observers would say, "Yes, that is the scene," because it would be recognizably the same; but it would not be exactly the same, and the amount of difference would depend on the disparity between their habitual ways of perceiving.

Let us say that one of our observers is interested in stargazing in general and can pick out constellations. The other has never bothered to learn the names or locations of most of the constellations, but he is mildly interested in navigation, and he at least knows how to find the North Star. His eyes and his mind are guided automatically along the line of pointer stars of the Big Dipper and reach for the pole star, *Polaris.* The heavens seem to him to converge at that point. The other person finds his eye drawn to the same region of the sky by the constellation *Ursa Major,* the Great Bear, and to him the North Star is simply a point of light near the tail of *Draco,* the Dragon. To the one, the Great Bear is a jumble of stars which he can, with some effort, force into a pattern. To the other, it is a bear, and his friend's Big Dipper is lost in the shoulder of the bear. "Do you see yonder cloud that's almost in shape like a camel?" asks Hamlet, and Polonius, eager to please, says, ". . . it's like a camel, indeed." "Methinks it is like a weasel," teases the prince, and the old man answers, "It is backed like a weasel." "Or like a whale?" asks Hamlet. "Very like a whale," says Polonius, because he has learned to see what he is supposed to see.

No society has existed which did not need a structure, a system of belief, by which it could ask and answer questions about its relationship to the universe. No age is without its myths because myths are stories through which the age can see itself. Some ancient civilizations thought the gods brought rain as a reward to faithful people or withheld it as punishment. The human need to wonder made them create a religion, a mythic system, that included a rain god, and so they saw themselves in relation to their environment. They did not say to themselves, "This is a myth by which we will interpret our relationship to phenomena"; they embraced the myth as a true picture of the world. It was not the only picture, nor did it prove a satisfactory picture for later ages, when the means of observation or the vantage point for observing the world changed, but it was a workable picture all the same. The enduring truth was that the people prospered or suffered because of the presence or absence of rain; later ages changed the picture and the names of the agents or gods, but not the truth behind the picture and not the need to make myths of their own.

In the largest sense, it does not matter at all how devout a believer Homer was in the tales he related about gods and goddesses. Perhaps he viewed the tales themselves philosophically, assuming they were vehicles by which man might catch a glimpse of the nature of divinity. I think it probable, though, that he believed in all the gods—in Proteus, the old shape-shifter, in the earth-shaker Poseidon, in Ares, and in Aphrodite. No one who knew as much about the sea and the land as Homer did could doubt the existence of the first two, and anyone who could doubt the powers of Ares and Aphrodite—by whatever names—simply has never known the full range of human emotions. The myths (the tales, the names of the gods) were just workable pictures of man's relationship to observable phenomena.

Not only must an age have a mythic structure, it must take that structure seriously. The moment it begins to call one structure into question it begins immediately to build another; the second structure then becomes the picture of the world, and the first is relegated to the rank of a curiosity. A myth is not an erroneous picture of the world; it is just a picture. Someday, of course, our own myths will be curios, mementos of the twentieth century, and students of mythology will study them and wonder how grown-ups could believe such childish tales. To doubt this is to doubt that human society will change as it has changed over hundreds of centuries. Our pictures of time, of necessity, of the nature of relationships between human beings, even of the nature of matter, are constantly being called into question, and so our myths are subtly changing.

In the West, our ways of perceiving the world have changed so radically and so many times in the last two centuries that the traditional mythic structure that worked admirably for hundreds of years is now in tatters. Each new major discovery in science and mathematics occasioned a gradual reworking of philosophical approaches to the world, and the inevitable result was always a challenge to the dominant mythology. This is not simply a case of science versus religion. It is instead a case of change in means of perception so pervasive and dramatic and rapid that the truths of one generation are regarded as rank superstition by the next, and in every generation society is threatened by the absence of tales and traditions by which it can know itself. Men have lived, and done so richly and resourcefully, without a belief in gods, but it is difficult to imagine anyone living a meaningful life without believing in anything at all. If a man does not believe in the efficacy of prayer, he has plenty of company in the modern world. But if he does not believe in the efficacy of action, or meditation, or knowledge, or anything at all, then he is a lonely nihilist, and his world has no meaning.

If we can do without tales of the gods, we cannot do without tales of heroes and villains, of monsters and the human courage it takes to face them. Those tales are the myths we live by, because they show us that life means something after all. The names of the monsters change, and so do those of the heroes and of the struggle itself as our ways of perceiving the world change, but every society must have its heroes and its monsters— perhaps some gods, too, if it can afford them—because it must find meaning in the world.

The study of mythology is not like the study of science, history, or literature. (It is closest, in some ways, to the study of literature.) It is the study of ways of seeing the world, ways of organizing and finding meaning in all the disparate facts that have always surrounded every man and woman in every civilization. We cannot understand any society very well until we understand something about its mythology. The same could be said about understanding an individual. We might ask, "What does he do for a living?" or "What does he look like?" or "Where was he born?" or a hundred other common questions that would tell us very little about the man. But if we could ask, "What does he believe in?" or "What does

he value?" or "Who are his heroes?" and if we could receive answers to
those questions, then we would know the man himself and not just some
facts about him.

Ever since the eighteenth century, there have been enthusiasts who
have insisted that the Western world was on the verge of some sort of
spiritual rebirth, a revision of the values by which a civilization lives.
Some of them, caught up in the excitement over technological advances
and the achievements of the scientific method, have suggested that the
road to spiritual renewal must lead to total abandonment of strictly
religious attitudes since religion itself was merely a holdover from a dark
and superstitious age. Enlightenment must come through the proper
application of man's energies—in science, technology, and the social
sciences. There is hope, after all, that man himself (and not the gods) can
abolish war, hunger, poverty, and all the other scourges to his own
happiness.

In sharp reaction to this championing of the power of pure reason
are those who insist that man must return to a belief in the supernatural,
to traditional Protestantism or Catholicism, for instance, in order to be
reborn. They see as the only hope for the future a reembracing, not only
of the traditional religious values, but also of the traditional religious
mythical structure. Between these two warring extremes we find a large
number of people who are quite unable to accept as meaningful the
traditions of their religion, and yet find strict rationalism and materialism
a sterile and unsatisfactory guide for living. In a translator's preface to Carl
Jung's *Modern Man in Search of a Soul,* Cary F. Baynes says that these
people "have outgrown the Church as exemplified in Christianity, but . . .
have not therefore been brought to deny the fact that a religious attitude
to life is as essential to them as a belief in the authenticity of science."
They believe in what Baynes (following Jung) calls "the soul," but they
cannot find proper expression for their belief in either traditional theology
or in materialism: "They do not wish to sever the real piety they feel
within themselves from the body of scientific fact to which reason gives

its sanction."[3]

Man embraces myths because he must. His mind seeks order everywhere in the universe, and if it cannot find order ready-made, it will impose order and believe in the order it has imposed. Man will take seriously—will regard as true, at least in a sense—those tales which reflect and reinforce the order he has imposed. Thus he will make in stone or clay, in a cave in prehistoric Europe, an image of the eternal female, the sex goddess, and he will make her again in a different form in ancient Greece, and again in the Indus valley. He will make the eternal mother, the weeping Demeter mourning her daughter's loss, or the anguished Mary watching the descent from the cross. He will make the hero, the Herakles or Beowulf or Cuchalain or Odysseus. He will contemplate the end of things, when the four horsemen ride or when the wolf Fenrir kills Odin, and the gods themselves face destruction. The tales are a way of dealing with realities which are no less pressing because they are distant instead of strictly contemporary, or because they are metaphysical or spiritual rather than material.

When, in the fifth book of *Paradise Lost,* Adam asks Raphael to tell him about warring angels and the fall of Satan, Milton almost makes the archangel scratch his head in perplexity as he replies,

> High matter thou injoin'st of me, O prime of men,
> Sad task and hard, for how shall I relate
> To human sense th' invisible exploits
> Of warring Spirits; how without remorse
> The ruin of so many glorious once
> And perfet while they stood; how last unfold
> The secrets of another World, perhaps
> Not lawful to reveal? Yet for thy good
> This is dispens't, and what surmounts the reach
> Of human sense, I shall delineate so,
> By lik'ning spiritual to corporal forms,
> As may express them best.

---

[3]Cary F. Baynes, "Preface" to C. J. Jung, *Modern Man in Search of a Soul* (New York: Harcourt, Brace, and Company, n.d.), pp. ix-x.

Raphael rises to the task, of course, knowing that if Adam is going to be able to deal with spiritual truths at all, he will probably be able to deal with them best in the form of stories. Raphael tells "the prime of men" a myth because through the myth Adam might be able to deal with the truth.

All myths do the same thing: they attempt to relate man in some meaningful way to the goings-on of the universe. They reflect a world that is meaningful and orderly and, when they are outgrown because man's ideas about order have changed, they have to be discarded or altered and new myths must replace them. Not all myths involve theology directly, of course, but the ones which do, attempt to relate the individual life to the infinity of possibilities from which life springs. Our lives—all our individual lives—are like bubbles on the surface of a pond or lake; they form, float, and burst, but still there is the water underneath that sustains more bubbles and has given rise to all the bubbles in the past. The myths deal with the individual and the universal, the finite and the infinite—the bubbles and the lake, to extend a homely metaphor.

Many traditions (for example, the Judaic, the Christian, and the Islamic) not only make the bubbles conscious of the lake; they make the lake conscious of the bubbles, too. A few other traditions (like Zen Buddhism) do not posit the existence of a conscious infinity at all; their function is only to make the bubbles properly aware of the lake from which they arise and to which they must return. Water to water, to paraphrase another text. All traditions must somehow make sense of the finitude of bubbles. That is one of the functions of myth and of ritual.

We partake of life through myth and ritual; the words or actions used link us symbolically with the lake beneath us. We are no longer, for the moment, individual lives only, but a part of something older and larger than ourselves, a part of the infinity of possibilities. We are always aware of our individual existences, when we talk or work, argue or laugh, or in any way exercise our individuality. We feel the dark water beneath us, though, in the awed silence of ritual and in the best stories about gods and heroes. The rituals might be communal and complex, as in a church worship, or they might be individual and simple, as in eating a fish that one has caught and cleaned himself. Either way, something is touched — sometimes through words, but always beyond words, because the roots of what is touched are older than language: they are the same age as fear and wonder.

Seen this way, the dome on St. Paul's has precisely the same power to move and to excite awe as the ruined columns of the temple of Apollo at Delphi. Here, one says, is what happens when man feels the force, the age, and power of Life beyond or beneath the individual life and is driven by what he feels to create a structure that will reinforce that feeling for himself and for others. Perhaps Apollo never walked around at the Aereopagus in Athens and sat at the trial of Orestes, as Aeschylus claimed he did. Apollo, the beautiful god of light, enlightenment, poetry, the most "Greek" of all the gods, was certainly real enough; and he will be real as long as a single stone remains on top of another stone at Delphi, and as long as just one person visiting that heap of broken columns can feel the hair rise on the back of his neck and be struck to silence. Perhaps no one ever really rose from the dead, but Christ is real enough at Saint Paul's and will be so as long as people worship there. One comes into contact, at such places — but not just at such places — with the life beneath the individual life, and so the myths are as true then as anything needs to be. Certainly they are as true as bubbles that wink and break in sunlight and vanish as if they had never been seen.

Joseph Campbell tells a story about a woman who came to see a great Hindu guru. The woman said, "I find I don't love God. I've tried to convince myself that I do, but I don't." The guru asked, "Is there nothing in the world that you love?" and the woman answered, "Yes, I love my nephew." "Well," said the guru, "and there He is." Something lasts, something is real — even if we must call it only a lake of possibilities — and it doesn't matter what tales or what rituals we use to feel that presence.

If some of the tales from the Judeo-Christian tradition never die, it will be because their ability to touch the deeper reaches of being never fades: the whole story of the fall (repeated over and over again in every religion), touching the truth of man's individuality, his longing for community and permanence, his liability to temptation and pride, and his fear of death; Job sitting on his filthy hill asking for reasons, and a voice out of a whirlwind telling him that the final knowledge is acceptance of the irrational, that sometimes there aren't any reasons—as terrifying as that knowledge is; and the writer in Ecclesiastes looking at the whole cycle of man and the seasons and realizing, as if for the first time, that though "one generation passeth away, and another generation cometh," yet "the earth abideth forever," and "the sun also ariseth, and . . . all the rivers run into the sea, yet the sea is not full." These are expressions of a religious mood, a feeling that looks beyond the bubbles to their source and their destiny, finding a kind of community and a kind of peace in that.

If we have lost, for reasons having to do with our changed perspectives on the world, an ability to make once-viable traditions seem anything more than dead collections of tales, that is not an indication that we are without myths. We are between myths—reaching sometimes backwards toward what we thought we knew, sometimes forwards into what we do not yet know—in an effort to find stories that will define us to ourselves. Futuristic fantasy, science fiction, new directions in theology or philosophy[4]—even new directions in the social and natural sciences— all go to make up a mythic background, a field of possibilities which might be shaped by some future Homer or Hesiod or Moses into a coherent pattern. In the meantime, we create order as we can, watching ourselves and our world sometimes in broken bits and pieces of tales, as we might study our reflections in the pieces of a shattered mirror. We might scorn the mirror's fragility (it was only glass), but we cannot help but be struck by how the larger pieces show us what we seek and shun, and we wonder how we will replace it.

---

[4]For a discussion of the "noosphere" of Teilhard de Chardin as myth, see Raphael Patai, *Myth and Modern Man* (Englewood Cliffs NJ: Prentice Hall, 1972), p.p. 61-65 and 306-11.

Index

Adam, 2, 54, 61
Aeschylus, 5, 7, 70, 119
African mythology, 107-11
Agave, 7
Alcott, Bronson, 10
Aphrodite, 114
Apollo, 7, 119
Ares, 114
Aristotle, xi, 18, 41
Arnold, Matthew, 81
Arthur, 68
Astarte, 44
Atreus, 5
Auden, W. H., 42
Augustine, 8

Baal, 44
Bacchus, 45
Baldyr, 111
Bantu myths, 107-11
Barlowe, Joel, 61n
Barnett, Lincoln, 40, 41
Barrett, William, 2, 2n, 37, 37n, 52n
Baynes, Cary F., 116-17

Beowulf, xi, 16, 117
Blake, William, 55, 70
Boccaccio, Giovanni, 8
Bohr, Niels, 40
Bradford, William, 52, 54
Brahma, 60
Brahman, 60
Bronowski, Jacob, 24n, 40, 118
Brown, Charles Brockden, 54
Browning, Robert, 32-36
Brooks, Cleanth, 72, 73, 89n
Bruno, Giordano, 27, 27n, 28, 29
Bultmann, Rudolf, 32
Burroughs, Edgar Rice, 49-50
Bryon, George Gordon, 70, 99

Campbell, Joseph, x, 1, 14-15, 15n, 21, 21n, 118, 119
Camus, Albert, 2, 20, 31
Carter, Jimmy, 72-73
Cassirer, Ernst, 84-85
Castro, Fidel, 70
Chardin, Pierre Teilhard de, 120n
Charlemagne, xi

Clement of Alexander, 8
Coleridge, Samuel, *55*
Communism, 73n, 85-90
Conrad, Joseph, 49, *74-75*
Constantine, 47
Cook, J. D., 8n
Copernicus, Nicolas, 24, 29, 31, 41
Crystal Palace, 29
Cuchulain, 117
Cupid, 46

Dante Alighieri, 8
Darwin, Charles, 29, 30
Darwinism, 48-49
Delphi, 46, 119
Demeter, 44, 117
Democritus, 41
Dickens, Charles, 94
Diderot, Denis, 10
Dionysus, 7, 46, 47
Donne, John, 20
Dos Passos, John, 89
Durga, 60
Dylan, Bob, 61

Eddas, 15
Eddington, A. S., 40, 40n
Einstein, Albert, 39-41
Eliade, Mircea, x, xn, 87-88
Eliot, T. S., 20, 37-39, 49, 59
Elizabeth I, 28-29
Emerson, Ralph Waldo, *55*, 56, 57, 83, 88
Enceladus, 10
Engels, Friedrich, 86-90
Enlightenment, 51-52, 89
Erinyes, 5, 7
Euhemerism, 8, 45
Euhemerus, xi, 7
Euripides, 6, 7

Faded dieties, 45
Faulkner, William, 20, 50, 62n, 95
Fenrir, 117
Fitzgerald, F. Scott, 20
Flood story, 16-18
Folktale, 6
Ford, Henry, 94
Foscarini, Paolo, 27
Franklin, Benjamin, 51, *55*
Frazer, Sir James George, 13, 13n

Freud, Sigmund, ix, x, 11-12, 12n
Frost, Robert, 80-82

Galileo Galilei, 23-28, 29
Gann, Lewis H., 108
Genesis, 16, 17, 18, 30
Gilgamesh Epic, 17-18
Gotterdammerung, 15
Grail, the, 68, 82
Guevara, Che, 70

Harrison, Jane, 13, 13n
Hawthorne, Nathaniel, 57, 62n
Heisenberg, Werner, 41
Hemingway, Ernest, 3, 20, 31, 42, 50, 95
Hera, 43, 44
Herakles, 117
Herodotus, 7
Hesiod, 6, 7, 46
Hieros gammos, 43-44
Higher criticism of the Bible, 31
Hirohito, 66
Hitler, Adolf, 66
Ho Chi Minh, 66
Hogins, James Burl, x, 12n
Homer, xi, 7, 43, 46, 114

Ishtar, 44
Islam, 45

James, William, 96
Jefferson, Thomas, 51, 88
Jove, 45, 46
Jung, Carl, ix, x, 12-13, 13n, 15, 101, 116

Kali, 60
Kepler, Johannes, 25n
King, Martin Luther, Jr., 70

Lafitau, Pere Joseph, 9
Lasch, Christopher, 103
Leda, *5*
Lenin, V. I., 90
Levi-Strauss, Claude, 14, 14n
Lewis, R. W. B., 52n, 72, 73, 82n, 94-95
Lovejoy, Arthur O., 24, 25, 25n, 26n
Lowell, Robert, 65
Lyell, Charles, 30

Macleish, Archibald, 39
Malinowski, Branislav, 13

Mars, 46
Marx, Karl, 85-90
Maya, 60
Mayerson, Phillip, 7, 9n
Melville, Herman, 10, 57, 95, 99
Mhondoro, 110
Milton, John, 20, 26, 39, 117
Musikavanhu, 109
Mythology,
    Akkadian and Babylonian, 17-18
    and folklore, 6
    as language, 18-19
    Bantu, 107-11
    Christian, Judeo-Christian, 2, 8-9, 16-18,
        44-47, 119-20
    Hindu, 59-62
    importance of, 15-21
    Norse, 15-16
    Romano-Greek, 43-47
    study of, 6-15
    vitality of, 5-6, 119-20

Nanga, 109-10
Neanderthal man, 91-92
New Beginning, the, 54-57, 61-75, 89
Newton, Sir Isaac, 41
Nietzsche, Friedrich, 2, 36-37, 41
Nihilism, 2, 37

Odin, 117
Odysseus, 117
Orestes, 5, 119
Ovid, 45-46

Paine, Thomas, 10, 51
Parker, Theodore, 10
Parvoti, 60
Pascal, Blaise, 23, 31
Patai, Raphael, 7, 8, 120n
Paul, 46
Peirce, Charles S., 96
Pentheus, 7
Percival, 68
Persephone (Proserpina), 11, 44
Perseus, 10
Phaedra, 111
Phaeton, 9
Plato, 41
Pol Pot, 66
Poseidon, 114

Pound, Ezra, 20
Pragmatism, 96-99
Prometheus, 8, 10, 111
Ptolemy, 20, 24-26
Psyche, 46
Pythagoras, 6

Ragnarok, 15, 61
Raleigh, Sir Walter, 1
Rand, Ayn, 99-100
Reed, John, 89
Richards, I. A., 49
Roheim, Geza, 6
Rousseau, Jean Jacques, 54
Rutherford, Ernest, 40

Sartre, Jean Paul, 20, 31, 51-52, 105
Seznec, Jean, 8n
Shakespeare, William, 24, 33, 100, 107, 113
Shakti, 60
Shelley, Percy, 49-50
Shenker, Israel, 24n, 27
Shiva, 60, 62
Southey, Robert, 55
Stein, Benjamin, 71n
Stevens, Wallace, 77-80
Strauss, D. F., 31
Swinburne, Algernon Charles, 11

Tennyson, Alfred, 30-31, 48, 49-50
Thales, 6
Theagenes of Rhegion, 6
Thoreau, Henry David, 43, 55, 57
Tillyard, E. M. W., 28, 28n
Tocqueville, Alexis de, 94
Tolkien, E. M. W., 15-16, 16n
Twain, Mark, 3, 83, 91, 96-99

Ussher, James, 30

Vadzimu, 109
Vergil, 8
Vietnam War, 65-66
Villain, mythic, 71n
Vishnu, 59
Volsungasaga, 15
Voltaire, 10

Warren, Robert Penn, 72, 73, 82n
Wayne, John, 95
Whitman, Walt, 54, 55-57, 61, 68

Wordsworth, William, 10, 11, 49
Wolfe, Tom, 70-71
World War I, World War II, 64-65

Yeats, William Butler, 45, 47-48

Zeus, 5, 43, 44, 111
Zimbabwe, Shona beliefs in, 109-11

MYTH AND MEANING, MYTH AND ORDER

Interior Design by Haywood Ellis
Binding Design by Margaret Jordan Brown

Composition by Omni Composition Services, Macon, Georgia
     The text was typeset on an Addressograph Multigraph Comp/Set 5404, then paginated on an A/M
     Comp/Set 4510.

Design and production specifications:
     typeface—13/15 Weiss
     text paper—60 pound Warren's Old Style
     endpapers—Multicolor Antique, Muscatel
     cover—Holliston Roxite B51508
     dust jacket—100 pound enamel, printed three colors (PMS 871 gold metallic, PMS 208 opaque
          burgundy, and PMS opaque black), and varnished.

Printing (offset lithography) was by Omnipress, Inc., Macon, Georgia
Binding by John H. Dekker and Sons, Grand Rapids, Michigan